Editor-in-Chief and Founder:
Lyndon H. LaRouche, Jr.
Editorial Board: *Lyndon H. LaRouche, Jr. , Helga Zepp-LaRouche, Robert Ingraham, Tony Papert, Gerald Rose, Dennis Small, Jeffrey Steinberg, William Wertz*
Co-Editors: *Robert Ingraham, Tony Papert*
Technology: *Marsha Freeman*
Transcriptions: *Katherine Notley*
Ebooks: *Richard Burden*
Graphics: *Alan Yue*
Photos: *Stuart Lewis*
Circulation Manager: *Stanley Ezrol*

INTELLIGENCE DIRECTORS
Economics: *Marcia Merry Baker, Paul Gallagher*
History: *Anton Chaitkin*
Ibero-America: *Dennis Small*
Russia and Eastern Europe: *Rachel Douglas*
United States: *Debra Freeman*

INTERNATIONAL BUREAUS
Bogotá: *Miriam Redondo*
Berlin: *Rainer Apel*
Copenhagen: *Tom Gillesberg*
Lima: *Sara Madueño*
Melbourne: *Robert Barwick*
Mexico City: *Gerardo Castilleja Chávez*
New Delhi: *Ramtanu Maitra*
Paris: *Christine Bierre*
Stockholm: *Ulf Sandmark*
United Nations, N.Y.C.: *Leni Rubinstein*
Washington, D.C.: *William Jones*
Wiesbaden: *Göran Haglund*

ON THE WEB
e-mail: eirns@larouchepub.com
www.larouchepub.com
www.executiveintelligencereview.com
www.larouchepub.com/eiw
Webmaster: *John Sigerson*
Assistant Webmaster: *George Hollis*
Editor, Arabic-language edition: *Hussein Askary*

EIR (ISSN 0273-6314) *is published weekly
(50 issues), by EIR News Service, Inc.,
P.O. Box 17390, Washington, D.C. 20041-0390.
(703) 297-8434*

European Headquarters: E.I.R. GmbH, Postfach Bahnstrasse 9a, D-65205, Wiesbaden, Germany
Tel: 49-611-73650
Homepage: http://www.eir.de
e-mail: info@eir.de
Director: Georg Neudecker

Montreal, Canada: 514-461-1557
eir@eircanada.ca

Denmark: EIR - Danmark, Sankt Knuds Vej 11, basement left, DK-1903 Frederiksberg, Denmark.
Tel.: +45 35 43 60 40, Fax: +45 35 43 87 57. e-mail: eirdk@hotmail.com.

Mexico City: EIR, Sor Juana Inés de la Cruz 242-2 Col. Agricultura C.P. 11360
Delegación M. Hidalgo, México D.F.
Tel. (5525) 5318-2301
eirmexico@gmail.com

Copyright: ©2018 EIR News Service. All rights reserved. Reproduction in whole or in part without permission strictly prohibited.

Canada Post Publication Sales Agreement #40683579

Postmaster: Send all address changes to *EIR*, P.O. Box 17390, Washington, D.C. 20041-0390.

Signed articles in *EIR* represent the views of the authors, and not necessarily those of the Editorial Board.

81 Days that Will Change the World

90 Days to Make
A Breakout for All Ages

Aug. 9—The U.S. midterm elections are less than 90 days away. In these 90 days, the present British coup against the President can be thoroughly and roundly defeated, and the basis for a New Bretton Woods agreement between the Presidents of the United States, Russia, China, and the government of India put into place—the remedy proposed by Lyndon La-Rouche for routing the British Empire once and for all.

If, however, the present Democratic Party prevails in the elections, then the Congressional effort to destroy the agents of the coup will be ended, and will be replaced by an impeachment proceeding against Donald Trump. History will be on a different world-line.

Those are the stark alternatives we face, as do the populations of the four nations which could implement LaRouche's proposal. We have the unique potential to turn this battle in the right direction, but the clock is now ticking, and actual leadership, modeled on that of Lyndon LaRouche, is what we must now summon.

Never before in human history have the British stood so exposed. There have been further revelations in the last days about Christopher Steele's paid role with the FBI beginning in February 2016, and his continuing relationship with Bruce Ohr and the Obama Justice Department hierarchy. It now stands fully exposed how they have aimed squarely at bringing down this President now. As Rudy Giuliani, one of the President's lawyers, said yesterday, the Mueller investigation is going to blow up, and the law enforcement focus is going to turn to those responsible for this corrupt witch-hunt. It's our job to point out that all roads lead to the conclusion that this has been a full-scale British subversion operation against the United States.

EIR Contents

www.larouchepub.com   Volume 45, Number 33, August 17, 2018

Fish Stinks from the Head Down: An Update on the Mueller Inquisition

by Barbara Boyd

Aug. 9—The question to be answered here is, to which "head" do we refer, when citing this ancient cross-cultural metaphor in our headline? We have insisted, since we began covering the continuing regime change operation in the United States, that the "head" is the Anglo-Dutch imperial system, whose capital is the City of London and whose leading colonial administrators here in the United States, were led most recently by Barack Obama and those he chose to run his intelligence agencies: John Brennan, James Comey, and James Clapper. The torso associated with this "head" here in the United States includes the establishment wing of the Republican Party and the neo-conservatives, who, through such institutions as the American Enterprise Institute and the Koch Brothers, are fonts of British geopolitical schemes. The Anglo-Dutch Empire is the entity which has dedicated its intelligence agencies, its controlled media, its think tanks and foundations, Hollywood and all of its other institutions engaged in manipulating mass popular opinion, and its bought-and-paid-for Senators and Congressmen, to removing Donald Trump from the Presidency, by whatever means necessary.

Trump has completely and repeatedly enraged them by laughing off their power and taking his case directly to the people, ridiculing these "elites" publicly in front of mass audiences, and by threatening to produce a world in which China, Russia, the United States, and similar rational populations fully develop the econo-

The leading British colonial administrators in the United States (left to right) John Brennan, James Comey, James Clapper, and their hitman (below) Special Counsel Robert Mueller.

mies of the world.

According to reliable reporting, the President is also engaged in serious discussions with Vladimir Putin about eliminating nuclear weapons, while maintaining the technological capacities of both Russia and the United States. This is a policy—like the Lyndon LaRouche/Ronald Reagan Strategic Defense Initiative—which the British view as a mortal threat to the financial containment, regime change, and information warfare operations by which they maintain their power. Special Counsel Robert Mueller is simply the designated amoral legal assassin for this imperial entity, the blunt instrument by which Donald Trump is to be delivered for impeachment, if all goes as planned, at the conclusion of the 2018 U.S. midterm elections.

Trump has been so mercilessly targeted because he threatens to end the decades-long reign of terror, poverty, and endless war emanating from the deliberate destruction of Franklin Roosevelt's Bretton Woods system in August 1971, and the founding of the new speculative Anglo-Dutch Empire on its ruins. As LaRouche's *Executive Intelligence Review* has exclusively documented, after the destruction of Bretton Woods, these newly emboldened imperialists set out to deliberately cause the "controlled disintegration" of the advanced sector's physical economies under a plan specifically articulated by British economist Fred Hirsch and confessed in the CFR "Project 1980s" documents produced by the New York Council on Foreign Relations.[1] The physical hollowing out of the United States economy, the outsourcing of our productive economy to China, Mexico, and other countries whose economies we attempted

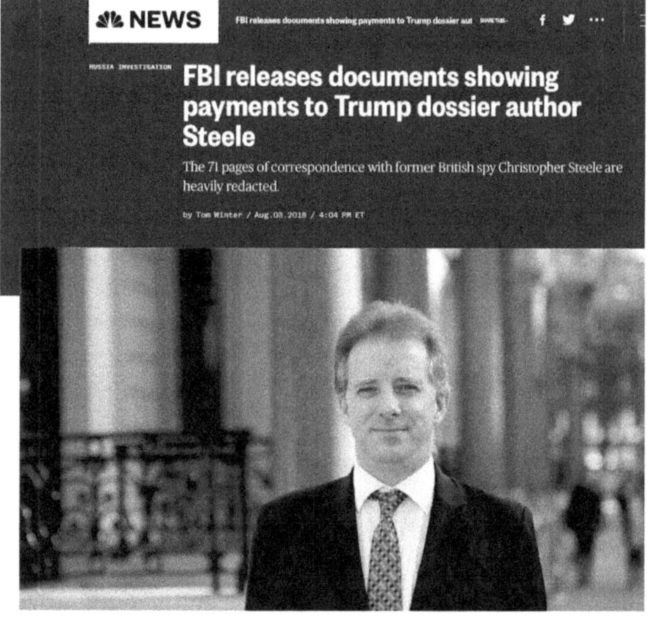

to freeze in cheap labor manufacturing, raw materials extraction, or worse—all of these horrors flow from the system which Donald Trump now threatens to overthrow.

Popular ignorance is our enemy's chief weapon in this war. Some in the Trump movement, for example, proclaim themselves partisans of British free trade, not knowing that that was the central issue our American revolutionists had with the British. Some in the Trump movement claim that the City of London/Wall Street monetary enslavement of the economy is a "free market" and mistake dirigism for socialism, ignorant of Alexander Hamilton's economic mobilization policies which made good on the Revolutionary War debt, cre-

ated the infrastructure of our prosperous new republic, won both the Civil War and World War II, and resulted in decades of sustained economic growth. Some in the Trump movement utter jingoism against Russia and China, without recognizing that the same people who are out to remove the President would destroy these nations as well, because they, too, threaten to upset the "order" which has immiserated the world.

To put a fine point on how public relations bilge conceals and confuses, hiding the actual essence of people and institutions from those without the time to study them—in July 2018, the supposedly "right wing" and "pro-business" American Enterprise Institute and John Podesta's "left wing" "cradle of the Resistance," Center for American Progress, merged programs to unite against a common target—the "authoritarian populism" they ascribe to President Donald Trump.

In the same vein, aiming at nothing less than the "head" in the coup operation—the Anglo-Dutch imperial system—to totally dismantle it and send its human appendages, both in the U.S. and in Britain, to jail, is the only path to victory now. Otherwise, you will be stuck, shouting impotently, or, for purposes of pure political survival, making short-term pragmatic compromises within the present system. Such pragmatism, the mortal flaw of most politicians, according to Lyndon LaRouche, only promises death by a thousand cuts rather than in one spectacular blow.

Happily, new and explosive revelations in the last few weeks about the British and American actors in this coup, have brought us ever closer to exposing the "head" here, and beginning wholesale dismantlement. These include the revelation that Christopher Steele, the MI6 author of the anti-Trump dirty information warfare dossier financed by Hillary Clinton and the Democratic National Committee, and a major long-term asset of the Empire, was working as a human source for the FBI as of February 2016, if not earlier, well before the launch of the "official" FBI counterin-

---

1. See "A Conspiracy of Morons: the CFR Project 1980s" in the May 15, 1979 issue of *Executive Intelligence Review*.

Jonathan Winer (left photo), Assistant Secretary of State for European and Eurasian Affairs Victoria Nuland and Ukrainian coup leader, Andriy Parubiy.

Peter Strzok

telligence investigation of the Trump Campaign in late July 2016, and that Steele was in a back channel relationship with the number four official at the U.S. Department of Justice, Bruce Ohr, long after Steele was fired by the FBI in late October 2016, for his leaks to the news media.

The Steele/Ohr relationship lasted through May 2017 or later, according to documents recently obtained by Congress. After Donald Trump's election, Steele's work was funded, to the tune of $50 million, by George Soros, and by Tom Steyer and other Silicon Valley billionaires. These funders were seeking the President's impeachment. Christopher Steele and his British masters wanted Trump's impeachment also, but they had two motives. Their other motive was to mobilize U.S. public opinion to support the ongoing British destabilization and regime change operation against Vladimir Putin, in which Steele had been a major and continuous player since at least 2006.

These new revelations, and others, show that, by no later than late 2015, British intelligence was operating against the Trump campaign, feeding information to a task force convened by John Brennan at the CIA, and to Victoria Nuland and Jonathan Winer at the Department of State. Peter Strzok, the now notorious and biased lead FBI case agent on Russiagate, was the FBI's liaison to John Brennan, generally, and to John Brennan's anti-Trump task force specifically. John Brennan, of course, didn't blow his nose without reporting it to President Barack Obama. As we will detail below, it is now clear that the FBI's investigation of the Trump Campaign in 2016 was entirely predicated on British operations, conducted on foreign soil, and then laundered into the FBI through the CIA and the State Department. These operations were funded by the Clinton Campaign, the FBI, the CIA and other agencies of the United States, and various public and private entities in Britain.

To put what I just told you in boldface: A foreign government (the British), conducted entrapment operations on U.S. persons associated with an American presidential candidate (Donald Trump), on foreign soil (Great Britain), in coordination with the sitting President of the United States (Barack Obama) and his intelligence agencies, in order to fabricate a pretext for an FBI investigation, in which the target (Donald Trump) could be effectively defamed in the U.S. media as a Russian puppet, to wit, as implicitly engaged in treason against the United States. The President's favored candidate (Hillary Clinton) together with Obama's intelligence agencies, financed the entire operation.

After Donald Trump won the election, the same forces massed to create the basis for his impeachment, by the appointment of a known legal hitman, Robert Mueller, to take out the President. Mueller is well known for his abusive, *in terrorem* deployment of the prosecutorial power. His present effort to turn Paul Manafort into a liar against Donald Trump, for example, by overcharging a tax case in such a way as to threaten a sentence of 305 years in prison, would win admiring applause from the Spanish Inquisition's Tomas de Torquemada.

As Trump's lawyer Rudy Giuliani said on television Aug. 8, the whole Mueller investigation is about to blow, and instead of the President, the legal system is about to put its focus on Mueller, and the complicit Obama Administration officials who have run an actual criminal conspiracy against the United States. What Giuliani did not say, which is critical, is that this conspiracy was run on behalf of the British.

The new revelations come at a time when the Empire has set a variety of traps to box in the President concerning Russia, most recently in the wake of his historic and successful Helsinki summit with Vladimir Putin, and the insane response it provoked. On Wednesday, Aug. 8, the State Department announced new and horrendous sanctions against Russia based on a provable intelligence hoax—the discredited British Sergei Skripal poisoning, which the British government, without evidence, blames on Russia. This time Congressman Ed Royce, the bullethead, compromised, and as the retiring head of the House Foreign Affairs Committee, stepped forward as the Empire's useful idiot. He set into motion a legal process which seemed to require mandatory sanctions to be imposed by a U.S. State Department, which, for most of the period since Franklin Roosevelt's death, has been nothing but an adjunct of the British Foreign Office. Back in March, when the British generated this hoax, and Boris Johnson demanded NATO action against Putin, Trump had refused to jump to the ramparts. As we shall show, it is hardly accidental that Christopher Steele's Orbis Intelligence also shows up, front and center, in the British Skripal poisoning operation.

A Short History Lesson

As Professor Stephen Cohen has usefully elaborated, U.S. and Russian interference in each other's elections is hardly a new phenomenon. On the Russian side, it has existed since the founding of the Communist International in 1919; on the U.S. side, since Woodrow Wilson sent American troops to fight in the Russian Civil War.[2] President Bill Clinton notoriously threw millions of dollars into securing Boris Yeltsin's 1996 election win, including providing a team of American consultants. During the brighter times of our relationship, Russia vir-

Underwood & Underwood

Soldiers and sailors from many countries, including the U.S.A., parade in front of the Allies' Headquarters Building in Vladivostok, Russia, September 1918.

tually assured the survival of this nation, first in the Civil War and then in World War II. The most recent and intense sprint into the dynamic of the so-called "new Cold War," which began when Russians again asserted their sovereignty against the wholesale looting of their country by the Empire in the 1990s, dates from the 2012 election which sent Putin to the Presidency a second time. The British, along with the Project Democracy forces run out of Hillary Clinton's State Department, intervened in Russia's 2012 elections, encouraging street riots opposing Putin, and then claimed that he won only as the result of a massive vote-fraud.

The British hate Putin because he, like Trump, refuses to be caged by them. As soon as Putin ascended to the Presidency for the second time, the British used Bill Browder, the American exile who found a home in the City of London and British intelligence operations—together with Jonathan Winer of the State Department and U.S. Senators John McCain and Ben Cardin—to create the Magnitsky Act financial sanctions against Russia. These previously unprecedented financial sanctions against internal judicial and police actions in a foreign state, were based on Browder's completely fraudulent claim that his tax accountant, Sergei Magnitsky, had died a whistle-blower's death at the hands of the Russian government. In reality, as independent investigators such as Andrei Nekrasov have documented, Magnitsky assisted in a massive fraud

____

2. Professor Cohen was able to bring up these facts during a late-July appearance on CNN.

CC/Hudson Institute
Bill Browder

World Economic Forum/Benedikt von Loebell
Dmitri Alperovitch

conducted by Bill Browder against the Russian government. So, again, it is no accident that Bill Browder and Jonathan Winer re-appear as major figures in Russiagate. They are part of the same British intelligence apparatus which surrounds Christopher Steele, and which specializes in creating and selling fake tales and legends to the gullible for purposes of low intensity warfare.

In 2014, as part of the Obama Administration's military encirclement of Russia, the British and the U.S. State Department ran a coup against Viktor Yanukovych, the duly elected President of Ukraine and a client of Paul Manafort. While partisans of maintaining Ukraine's relationship with Russia battled with the neo-Nazis used by Victoria Nuland and her British friends as the shock troops in the coup, and which they later installed in the government, Crimea held a referendum, voting, once again, to become a part of Russia. Christopher Steele, the very same author of Trump dirt and the MI6 protégé of Sir Richard Dearlove, provided hundreds of intelligence memos directly to Victoria Nuland, Jonathan Winer, and John Kerry at the State Department, to advance the Ukraine coup. Outflanked in Crimea and in Eastern Ukraine, the British claimed that their setback was due to Putin's superior mastery of "hybrid warfare," a key component of which was modern information warfare techniques based on social media and press manipulation. It was impossible for the British, in their arrogance, to fathom that anyone would vote against

being terrorized or killed by neo-Nazis, or for remaining associated with Russia. When Crimea voted for the Russian alternative, the arrogant British and American coup-masters chalked it up to a Russian "disinformation" campaign.

To counter an alleged Russian advantage (in Hillary Clinton's words, the Russians were "eating our lunch" when it came to information warfare), in 2014 the British formed the 77th Military Brigade, dedicated to advanced propaganda techniques on behalf of NATO and British and American intelligence agencies. This later morphed into the NATO Centre for Strategic Communications, a font of British hybrid warfare operations against Russia. As with all information warfare, the task is to paint the adversary, in this case Putin, as the monster of the century, while presenting your side as just beyond Heaven on Earth. Since 2014, millions have been spent to pump out endless bilge about the Russian threat, while censoring any skepticism, let alone any actual Russian viewpoint on world events. This censorship and propaganda offensive now encompasses every legacy media institution in the advanced sector, and, more recently, as the result of Russiagate, all major social media platforms as well.

The Atlantic Council's Digital Forensics Lab was the first among many such operations in the U.S., and is actually a part of the NATO Centre for Strategic Communications. It receives major funding from the British

U.S. Army/Hubert D Delany, III
Lance Cpl. Abdulla Mohamed (middle), a British psy-ops soldier in the 77th Brigade, with U.S. soldiers in Allied Spirit VIII exercise, Hohenfels, Germany, Jan. 25, 2018.

government, and now, from Facebook. Again, it is no accident that Dmitri Alperovitch, who used his company CrowdStrike to author the "Russia hacked the DNC and John Podesta" hoax, is also a major player in the Digital Forensics Lab. Now, there are dozens of similar censorship and propaganda operations, including StopFake, PropOrNot, the State Department's new Global Engagement Center, and multiple offshoots of Mikhail Khodorkovsky's Institute of Modern Russia. As a result, it is not an exaggeration to state that the First Amendment to the U.S. Constitution is on life support. This is not because the controlled fake-news mandarins have been called out by President Trump as a danger to our Republic. Rather, the Anglo-American elites have determined that only censored propaganda can be safely offered to Americans. In their view, the rubes, rabble and deplorables who voted for Donald Trump need to have their minds sanitized lest they vote again for Trump or similar candidates.

Facebook recently hired the Atlantic Council Digital Forensics gang to police their platforms. This resulted in the banning of the popular, if completely obnoxious, Alex Jones, on the grounds that his speech is offensive. Speech in the United States, public discourse about public events, has never been censored under the U.S. Constitution, unless it creates an imminent danger of violence or physical harm. Nonetheless, the National Defense Authorization Act of 2016, sponsored by the Obama Administration and the anti-Russia, anti-China neanderthals in the U.S. Congress, allocated major funding to create the State Department's Global Engagement Center, a Big Brother censorship and government propaganda apparat no different from George Orwell's Ministry of Truth, as portrayed in his novel, *1984.*

In 2015 and 2016, the British establishment watched in horror as the Trump candidacy in the United States and Brexit in Britain, gathered momentum in angry populations that had never recovered from the Wall Street/City of London collapse and bailout of 2008. Rather than look in the mirror and repudiate the insane post-industrial, consumer societies they created, and a globalist order founded on population control and cheap labor, the British and their satraps in the United States chose to continue and deepen operations to destabilize Putin and Russia. They claimed that Russia's superior "hybrid" warfare techniques were responsible for Trump's victory, and have set off an utterly mindless

public domain

John Podesta, White House Chief of Staff to President Clinton, and Counselor to President Obama.

and increasingly violent hysteria in this country, worse than that of the McCarthy era. In Europe, they claimed a Russian plot to destroy the European Union, leading with the British Brexit vote. Again, not surprisingly, Christopher Steele authored a study in April 2016 about the alleged Europe plot, parading out the same bilge about Russian social media operations deepening and exacerbating social divisions, which the Senate Intelligence Committee proudly and fraudulently presented to the America public as the Senate's own, original work product.

To what end? French counterintelligence and security expert Paul Barril has said that the Empire set out to destabilize Putin and Russia, setting into motion a slow regime-change operation, beginning with the murder of the dissident Alexander Litvinenko in London in 2006. Russia was blamed for Litvinenko's polonium poisoning, following an investigation led by none other than Christopher Steele, who was Litvinenko's handler in MI6. Barril says the name of this operation is "Operation Beluga." Whether or not Barril is correct on the specifics, something like that is very surely operating here, and, as President Trump has appropriately warned, the operation risks a thermonuclear confrontation between the world's two nuclear powers—a confrontation the world will not survive.

The Russian Hack That Wasn't and the Move to Eliminate Julian Assange

The founding fake premise of the ongoing British-instigated coup against President Trump, and the chief legal ground for Robert Mueller's inquisition against the President, is the claim that the Russians hacked the Democratic National Committee and the Chairman of

Hillary Clinton's campaign, John Podesta, and provided the results to WikiLeaks, which published them beginning on July 22, 2016. Two days after the June 12, 2016 announcement by WikiLeaks founder Julian Assange that he had an upcoming release of "leaks" related to Hillary Clinton, the DNC announced that it had been hacked. The very next day, an online persona calling itself "Guccifer 2.0" made its appearance, and claimed to be the source for the WikiLeaks material on Clinton, claiming to have acquired it by hacking the DNC. Guccifer 2.0 helpfully released a series of five documents to accompany its claim, including a document that the DNC announced had been stolen.[3]

As most know, the trove of documents later published by WikiLeaks proved to be authentic, and showed that the DNC had systematically sabotaged Bernie Sanders' 2016 presidential primary campaign against Hillary Clinton. The documents also demonstrated Clinton's sordid subservience to Wall Street. As President Putin noted during his July 16 summit with President Trump, what the documents actually showed— what Clinton and her Democratic Party colleagues were doing to destroy Sanders—was more troubling for our nation than the source of the documents.

Within three days of Assange's June 12 announcement, CrowdStrike, the DNC computer security vendor hired by Perkins, Coie—the same law firm paying Christopher Steele—claimed that the Russians had hacked the DNC, thus painting any future releases from WikiLeaks with a "Russia-did-it" brush, making it possible to distract attention from the gross misconduct of Hillary Clinton and her DNC. Christopher Steele chimed in with memos in his dirty dossier, specifically claiming that Putin personally ordered the DNC hack, to advance Trump's campaign.

Dmitri Alperovitch, CrowdStrike's founder and the aforementioned Russian émigré Putin-hater otherwise ensconced at the Atlantic Council's Digital Research Lab, led the "investigation." According to the *Guardian*, the British had already warned the DNC that their computer system was compromised back in 2015. The FBI delivered similar early warnings. If you believe the DNC's account, nothing was done about this for months, until a DNC researcher named Alexandra Chulapa—who ran social media operations during the Ukraine coup and was working with Ukrainian intelli-

Cancillería del Ecuador
Julian Assange, WikiLeaks founder, published a trove of documents related to Hillary Clinton.

gence to discredit Paul Manafort—sounded the alarm in April 2016. Even then, CrowdStrike allegedly waited until June to act against the attack—hardly the actions of a presidential campaign under attack by what it believed to be an enemy foreign government. Incredibly, the FBI and the U.S. intelligence community simply adopted CrowdStrike's findings without ever forensically examining the DNC's computers. When the DNC denied the FBI access to their servers—the crime scene in this incident—James Comey's FBI, which we now know was preoccupied with exonerating Clinton from her email malfeasance, and was positively rabid about destroying the Trump candidacy, stood down, with no further inquiry needed.

If the DNC and Podesta were hacked by Russians, the NSA would have been able to demonstrate that fact through actual evidentiary proof, a point made repeatedly by former NSA Technical Director Bill Binney. No such proof was, or has yet been offered. Instead, the main document presented to the American public was the January 6, 2017 "assessment" by analysts handpicked by John Brennan, a major player in the outrageously illegal operation against Donald Trump.[4]

____

4. Guccifer 2.0 (G2) became a central element for blaming Russia for hacking the material later released by WikiLeaks. As its name suggests, WikiLeaks mainly publishes leaks, and for this reason, takes great care to prevent exposing the identities of its sources, who may face legal and other repercussions for revealing classified or private material. It was therefore quite unusual for G2 to appear publicly at all, and to claim to be the source via a hack. While G2 claimed to be a lone Romanian hacker, a series of obviously planted clues (the computer equivalent of monogrammed handkerchiefs) revealed, to the supposedly intrepid reporters and analysts who found them right on cue, that G2 was not Romanian, but actually—gasp!—Russian, and trying to cover his tracks. This G2

____

3. A thorough timeline of events is available on Adam Carter's website of Guccifer 2.0 analysis, g-2.space

LPAC/Jason Ross

Bill Binney, former NSA Technical Director.

State Department/Ron Przysucha

Mike Pompeo, CIA Director.

On July 24, 2017, Veteran Intelligence Professionals for Sanity (VIPS) members Ray McGovern and former NSA technical Director Bill Binney, with other members of the VIPS, published an analysis based on what has been the only independent forensic investigation conducted to date concerning the alleged DNC hack.[5] It concluded, on the basis of data transmission speeds, that the materials released by Guccifer 2.0 were consistent with a download or a leak, rather than any hack by the Russian government or anyone else.

Following media coverage of the VIPS study, then-CIA Director Mike Pompeo met with Binney, at President Trump's urging, to discuss his findings. Other critics, such as Scott Ritter, stepped forward at the same time, to convincingly debunk the so-called "intelligence community assessment," although on very different grounds than Binney and McGovern.

Going directly to the question of source, WikiLeaks founder Julian Assange has long maintained that the source was not a Russian or a state actor. And Assange's colleague, Ambassador Craig Murray, claims to have acted as an intermediary to receive, in person, the damning trove of DNC and Podesta documents from a non-Russian whistleblower.

Well before the VIPS critique, Julian Assange himself had stepped forward to open negotiations with the U.S. Justice Department in early 2017. As revealed by

John Solomon in *The Hill,* Assange had acquired the CIA's top secret, codeword-classified hacking tools, the Marble Framework, and was preparing to publish them. These were equivalent to the crown jewels of CIA cyber-warfare, as they provide tools for hacking by the CIA or its contractors, while attributing the hack to a foreign entity. Among the sophisticated tools in this program are tools for attributing hacks conducted by the CIA to the Russian government. In return for immunity, Assange offered to subject the CIA cyberwar materials to redaction to protect sources and methods prior to publication; to discuss the CIA's security vulnerabilities which led to WikiLeaks' obtaining the material; and to provide evidence to the U.S. government demonstrating that a Russian hack was not the source of the DNC and Podesta publications by WikiLeaks. According to documents produced by Solomon, the Justice Department was conducting serious negotiations with Assange's lawyer when the FBI's James Comey, and Comey's sidekick, Virginia Senator Mark Warner, intervened to kill any deal in February 2017. Needless to say, Robert Mueller has not interviewed either William Binney or Julian Assange.

On July 13, 2018, however, Mueller produced an indictment of twelve alleged Russian GRU military intelligence officers for hacking the DNC and Podesta, claiming that Guccifer 2.0 and the related DCLeaks site were GRU fronts. While Deputy Attorney General Rob Rosenstein emphasized that Mueller did not charge any American with *colluding* with the Russians, and that the hack did not impact the result of the 2016 election, Mueller's move had two purposes: wrecking the

---

persona has been central to both the January 6, 2017 Intelligence Community Assessment blaming Russia and to Robert Mueller's July 2018 indictment. It is therefore important to use any tools available to determine whether there is any evidence that G2 actually hacked the DNC.

5. "Was the 'Russian Hack' an Inside Job?," *Consortium News.*

Vox EXPLAINERS POLITICS & POLICY WORLD CULTURE SCIENCE & HEALTH MORE +

Read: Mueller indictment against 12 Russian spies for DNC hack

It comes days before President Trump's summit with Russian leader Vladimir Putin.

By Alex Ward | @AlexWardVox | alex.ward@vox.com | Jul 13, 2018, 12:30pm EDT

summit, just days away, between Trump and Putin, and reviving the now-discredited foundation for his own investigation—the alleged Russian hack of the DNC and Podesta.

Neither ploy really worked. The summit proceeded, albeit with demands from Trump's deranged opponents that he should publicly kick Putin to the ground at the summit, if Trump wanted to avoid being accused of outright treason back here in the United States. The indictment itself only produced further fodder for those thinking critically, including Vladimir Putin and Donald Trump. Putin's offer to make the accused GRU officers available for interrogation by Mueller in Russia, in exchange for the U.S. making Browder and other British agents similarly available, was greeted favorably by Trump, creating a predictable firestorm in the United States. My use of the term, "thinking critically" here, means that I think that Putin and Trump have access to information about what actually happened which has not yet been shared with the general public, information which could send the perpetrators of the coup straight to prison. Mueller's indictment itself admits that CrowdStrike was in, and modifying, the scene of the crime—the DNC computer server—not just for two weeks in June, as originally claimed, but through September 2016. Further, the indictment's meticulous and shiny detail is really only a more detailed version of CrowdStrike's original analysis.

Bill Binney notes that the indictment's detail does not reflect NSA materials or an inside Russian source, as some have speculated. "Those materials are classified and are subject to criminal penalties for disclosure under U.S. law," Binney emphasized to this reporter. They would never be revealed in such a tawdry fashion. Since no purported officer of the GRU will ever appear in an American court, the novel written by Mueller and Rosenstein, still lacking anything resembling convincing proof, will never actually be tested. Mueller's prior indictment against the St. Petersburg-based Internet Research Agency, which created a media frenzy continuing over several news cycles, concerned a measly $200,000 in Facebook ads, most of which occurred after the 2016 election. That indictment has been challenged in federal court by one of the indicted corporate defendants, much to Mueller's surprise and chagrin, in a criminal case which is ongoing in Washington, D.C.

So, with rationality about Russia, at least on President Trump's part, having survived yet another determined effort to completely destroy any potential relationship, and with serious doubt about the central premise of Mueller's investigation still intact, on July 31, British journalist Duncan Campbell intervened with a long-winded and wandering hit piece, published in the nondescript *Computer Weekly,* attacking participants in the VIPS analysis as Russian disinformation agents.

Campbell is considered to be the dean of British whistleblowers. He was the first to expose and name GCHQ, the British NSA. He was prosecuted under Britain's Official Secrets Act. He has otherwise exposed key aspects of Britain's surveillance programs. Lately, however, Campbell has re-fashioned himself to be an expert on Russian disinformation, teaching a course on it at Sussex University, and becoming deeply involved with the Consortium for Investigative Journalism. At the same time, he has developed a new coziness with GCHQ, and praised a "new openness" there under Robert Hannigan. Hannigan, of course, abruptly resigned his post right after Trump's election, a resignation which can be attributed to illegal spying against Trump by the British agency. And the Consortium for Investigative Journalism is funded by George Soros, Peter Omidyar, the Ford

Briton ran pro-Kremlin disinformation campaign that helped Trump deny Russian links

A British IT manager and former hacker from Darlington ran a disinformation campaign that duped former US intelligence agents and provided Donald Trump with manufactured "evidence" to deny that Russia interfered with the US election.

none needed

Duncan Campbell, famed British journalist and whistleblower, now cozy with GCHQ's Robert Hannigan, attempted to get Bill Binney to change his analysis concerning the alleged DNC hack.

Foundation and other public opponents of Donald Trump, and most famously published the "Panama Papers," a leak which many attribute to British intelligence and the CIA.

Campbell is also a personal friend of Bill Binney, and he invited Binney to Britain to review the Veteran Intelligence Professionals for Sanity (VIPS) research concerning the DNC hack. His article implies that Binney completely changed his analysis after conducting an independent review with his old friend, and that Binney had been snookered by Adam Carter and others who participated in the VIPS study and related forensics. When interviewed by this reporter on August 6th, however, Bill Binney was emphatic that he stood by the central conclusion of the VIPS study: "Guccifer 2.0" was a fabrication, and the DNC materials were downloaded, not hacked by the Russians. "The only thing I said I could not prove, was where the download occurred and by whom," Binney said. Binney noted that he cannot be held accountable for the mental derangement with which some of his friends, including some in the VIPS, have greeted his basic scientific inquiry. He noted that the only people who are really in a position to provide details about the "who and the where"

UK Government

Robert Hannigan, GCHQ Director, Nov. 2014 to Jan. 2017.

of the download, are Julian Assange and former Ambassador Craig Murray.

It is hardly coincidental then, that in the past weeks Assange has been threatened with eviction from the Ecuadorian Embassy in London where he was granted asylum after Sweden launched a prosecution against him. His access to computers, the Internet, or any form of communication have now been completely cut off by the Ecuadorian government. Both the British and the Americans stand ready to indict him. His friends say his health is going bad. WikiLeaks reported on August 8, that Assange has now been invited to appear before the Senate Intelligence Committee investigating Russiagate, at a time and place of his choosing. Given the stakes, there is every reason for the concern voiced by Assange's friends that his life is in imminent danger.

Christopher Steele's Perfidious True Crime Trail

It is now almost two years since the election of 2016. Over the course of those two years, through the diligence and tenacity of a few honest U.S. Congressmen and journalists, of Judicial Watch, and of intelligence community whistle-blowers on both sides of the Atlantic, and through the courage of President Trump, the brazen nature of the British interference in the 2016 election, and their all-out effort to force Trump from office has been forced into daylight. Christopher Steele and his mentor, Sir Richard Dearlove, are central players in the British plot, not just to retake the United States, but also to force regime-change in Russia based on a long-standing British hybrid warfare campaign. In addition to staging a coup against the President, they are attempting to recruit the entire population of the United States to this insane perspective against Russia. They have a long and storied history in creating fake news for political and strategic purposes, and running operations which leave a trail of bodies in their wake.

During the past week, we have learned that Steele was being paid as a human source by the FBI as early as February

2016, if not before, based on a release of his highly redacted FBI file to Judicial Watch in an FOIA suit. After he was fired as an official FBI human source in October 2016—based on the obvious fact that he was using his FBI relationship as coinage in the information-warfare operation he was running against Donald Trump for the British government, Barack Obama, and Hillary Clinton — his relationship with the FBI was continued through a back channel. That

Sir Richard Dearlove, KCMG, OBE, Chief of British Secret Intelligence, SIS/MI6, 1966-2004.

channel was the number four attorney at the U.S. Department of Justice, Bruce Ohr, whose wife, Nellie, worked for Steele's American employer, Fusion GPS, on the Trump Russiagate project.

According to documents finally released to Congress by the Justice Department, Ohr would meet with Steele, who would convey new "information," and then meet with the FBI to convey Steele's findings. This relationship lasted through May 2017, if not later. Ohr's meetings with the FBI were meticulously recorded on FD 302 forms by the FBI agents—the Deputy Associate Attorney General of the United States having become, in effect, an FBI informant, in order to circumvent Christopher Steele's firing as an informant for egregious violations of FBI Guidelines. Steele sought Ohr's intervention when Senators Lindsey Graham and Chuck Grassley referred him to the Department of Justice for prosecution, because of lies he told the FBI. Steele also sought Ohr's help in getting placed on Robert Mueller's investigative team. These entreaties were obviously based on the calculation that Ohr and others working with him were in a position to fulfill Steele's demands.

Stefan Halper

Previously, as the result of Congressional investigations and numerous British publications, we learned that the British were already warning John Brennan about Trump and the Russians as of late 2015, and that Brennan convened a task force at CIA headquarters no later than March 2016, to investigate the British claims and to launder them to the FBI. Brennan has stated that the British were screaming that Trump would "destroy the special relationship." The CIA is barred, generally, from U.S. domestic spying as a matter of law—let alone the completely illegal intervention into a U.S. presidential election which is at issue here.

As the result of the British/Obama Administration conspiracy, a whole slew of entrapment operations were set loose on British soil beginning in February-March 2016, targeting individuals loosely associated with the Trump campaign, specifically Carter Page and George Papadopoulos. A very sketchy character, the Maltese Professor Joseph Mifsud, who has multiple connections to British intelligence, targeted Papadopoulos during this period, providing him with a job, telling him that the Russians had Hillary's emails, and encouraging Papadopoulos to meet with various Russians introduced by Mifsud. Papadopoulos reported back to the Trump campaign what Mifsud told him, as well as what he was told by the Russian contacts to whom he was introduced, thus creating a documentary trail of fabricated "evidence."

CIA-MI6 asset Stefan Halper, a close friend of Sir Richard Dearlove, was recruited to repeatedly interrogate Carter Page and Papadopoulos about Russian

Carter Page

George Papadopoulos

Michael Flynn

"dirt" allegedly held by the Trump Campaign on Hillary Clinton, based on supposed collusion with the Russian government. The Australian High Commissioner to Britain, Alexander Downer—another player closely tied to Sir Richard Dearlove, Halper, the MI6-associated intelligence agency Hakluyt, and the Clinton Foundation—was set loose to get Papadopoulos drunk and induce confessions on the same topic, "Russian-generated dirt on Clinton" provided as a result of "collusion" with the Trump Campaign.

All of these story-lines and operations echoed claims that Christopher Steele was simultaneously making in his "dirty dossier" memos. These entrapment operations were intended to, and did, create a fabricated evidentiary trail, providing at least minimal credibility to the otherwise completely bogus and wild claims Steele was making in his dirty dossier, about Russia and Donald Trump. It appears that many of the results of these foreign operations were reported through State Department channels, including the U.S. Embassy in London, and then to the FBI. At the State Department, Victoria Nuland, the case officer for the Ukraine coup, and Jonathan Winer, were the early recipients of Steele's memos, and, according to them, they forwarded them to the FBI, while vouching for Steele's credibility. Winer also forwarded to the FBI memos from Clinton operatives Cody Shearer and Sidney Blumenthal, memos which he said buttressed claims made by Steele. At the same time, the same or similar communications were forwarded by Brennan's CIA to the FBI, including apparently, surveillance of the Trump Campaign conducted by GCHQ. Robert

Hannigan visited Brennan personally in the summer of 2016, to deliver, according to the *Guardian*'s accounts, a top secret, director-to-director briefing concerning Trump and Russia.

Halper, Dearlove, and Christopher Steele had targeted Defense Intelligence Agency (DIA) Director Lt. Gen. Michael Flynn as early as 2014, apoplectic that Flynn was calling out the Obama Administration and the Brits for supporting terrorists throughout the Middle East, and was seeking collaboration with Russia on destroying ISIS and similar terrorist groups. According to Chuck Ross of *The Daily Caller*, Halper falsely claimed that Flynn was compromised by a Russian woman, Svetlana Lokhova, and circulated this baseless and bogus claim throughout the British and U.S. news media in 2014. Many believe that Flynn was fired from the DIA by Barack Obama as the result of British complaints.

When the FBI opened its "official," "Crossfire Hurricane" investigation of the Trump Presidential campaign in July 2016, the immediate targets were Paul Manafort, Michael Flynn, George Papadopoulos, and Carter Page—all of the groundwork having been provided by operations conducted by a foreign government on foreign soil, in collaboration with Brennan's CIA and the State Department.

Manafort, whose unorthodox monetary dealings are no different from those of other swamp-like public relations gurus in Washington, D.C., committed the unforgivable sin of crafting Viktor Yanukovych's successful return to power in the Ukrainian elections, while the British and their Washington friends sought the opposite result in their ongoing destabilization campaign directed at Putin and the Russian state. In Manafort's case, the foreign government generating the evidence for his prosecution was most specifically the Ukrainian intelligence services, although a British role can in no way be discounted.

The June 2016 Trump Tower meeting, which has become such a focus of the news media and Robert Mueller again, is no different from the rest of these British-generated entrapment operations. Only the location for the operation, whose moniker was really "Planting Russian dirt about Hillary Clinton," was relocated from British soil to Trump's iconic home in Manhattan. Bill Browder, the British agent and the joint author, with his close friend Jon Winer, of the fake legend behind the Magnitsky Act, appeared for this operation as its putative scribe. He cited the Russian-American contingent accompanying the Russian lawyer Natalia Veselnitskaya to the Trump Tower meeting, and others, as unregistered foreign agents, in a complaint he promptly delivered to the U.S. Department of Justice after the meeting.

By October 2016, Carter Page had become the target of the first of four successive FISA surveillance warrants based on Steele's unverified memos, and on other fraudulent claims made by the FBI and Department of Justice to the FISA court—warrants which have shocked legal observers in the United States. This corrupt FISA operation, based on Christopher Steele's propaganda, was clearly aimed at turning Carter Page into a human microphone targeted at Donald Trump and his associates. According to Devin Nunes, Chair of the House Intelligence Committee, declassification of the 20 still-classified pages of the FISA warrant applications, will produce the largest shocks of all to an American public which is now focused on the major corruption in Obama's DOJ, FBI and other intelligence agencies.

Sir Richard Dearlove, KCMG, OBE, was Christopher Steele's boss as head of MI6 from 1999 to 2004. Steele and his business partner, Christopher Burrows, remain extremely close to Dearlove. By their own accounts, Sir Richard mentored and shepherded their calculated information warfare and legal entrapment operations against the Trump campaign. A major force in the U.S./British anti-Russian Henry Jackson Society of neo-conservatives, Sir Richard is widely blamed, correctly, for the fake intelligence that led the United States into the disastrous Iraq War.

Since the Litvinenko poisoning in 2006, the British have been in an all-out low-intensity war against the Russian state. Christopher Steele, who headed the Russian desk of MI6, has played a major role in all of these operations. According to Steele's own account, his firm, Orbis Business Intelligence, makes millions of dollars providing intelligence to warring Russian oligarchs, the perfect cover for disruption and low-intensity warfare. For example, the oligarch Oleg Deripaska, the Russian aluminum magnate who did business deals with Paul Manafort and later sued Manafort, is one of Steele's clients.

While deeply enmeshed in wrecking Donald Trump's campaign, Steele, by his own account to Jane Mayer, authored a study alleging a huge campaign of Russian interference in European elections with the goal of destroying the European Union—primarily aimed, no doubt, at Brexit and the "Leave" campaign. In April 2016, he claimed that the Kremlin was engaged in social-media warfare aimed at inflaming fear and prejudice, while it provided "opaque financial support" to favored politicians in the form of bank loans, gifts, and other kinds of support. Supposedly it specifically targeted Silvio Berlusconi and Marine Le Pen, as well as lesser-known right-wing nationalists in the United Kingdom and elsewhere. The Kremlin's long-term aim, the report concluded, was to "boost extremist groups and politicians at the expense of Europe's liberal democracies," according to Mayer's account in the *New Yorker*. Steele called his report "Operation Charlemagne."

Steele was the case officer who investigated the Alexander Litvinenko poisoning on behalf of MI6, immediately concluding that Russia had committed the spectacular murder, on specific orders from Putin, using polonium-210 as the poison. Prior to the poisoning, Steele ran Litvinenko, a defector from the Russian FSB, as an asset in Britain's destabilization operations against Putin and Russia. This murder was the opening shot of the war Britain has conducted against Putin since, with its intensity increased by orders of magnitude following the Ukraine coup.

Litvinenko worked for Russian oligarch Boris Berezovsky, who, after making millions looting Russia, fled to London and went to war against Putin on behalf of MI6. It is not a stretch to opine that Steele also ran Berezovsky's operations. Litvinenko was characterized

cc/John Armagh

Grave of Alexander Litvinenko at Highgate Cemetery, London, August 12, 2007.

as Berezovsky's "bomb thrower" against Putin. While the British authorities originally charged former FSB officer Andrei Lugovoi with the poisoning, and demanded his extradition, they did not charge the Russian state in the 2006 proceedings. This was despite claims that Litvinenko had made a death-bed statement blaming Putin for his murder, a sensational statement circulated world-wide by the British propaganda and public-relations apparat. That statement, it turns out, was drafted by another Berezovsky associate, Alex Goldfarb, a former employee of the infamous George Soros. The statement was further crafted by Bell, Pottinger, the disgraced British public relations firm famous for such contracts as its $540 million effort for the CIA making fake al-Qaeda propaganda films for the war in Iraq.

In the wake of the Ukraine coup, in May 2014, Theresa May, then Britain's Home Secretary, revived the Litvinenko case, purely for its propaganda value, eight years after his death. The revived review, lasting two years and ending in January 2016, ended up charging that Russia and Putin were "probably" responsible for the poisoning, in a report which used the word "probably" 35 times with respect to its major findings. Sir Robert Owen's report otherwise claimed that Andrei Lugovoi and another former Russian intelligence colleague of Litvinenko, Dmitry Kovtun, were responsible for the poisoning. The Owen report has proven to be highly controversial, even within Britain itself. Litvinenko's father, who still lives in Russia, blames the often violent operatives working with Berezovsky for his son's murder. Berezovsky himself apparently committed suicide by hanging in Britain in 2013.

When former MI6 double agent Sergei Skripal and his daughter Yulia were poisoned in Salisbury, England, in March 2016, the British and U.S. propaganda mills immediately announced that this was a repeat of the Litvinenko murder, this time using novichok, a widely-available nerve agent originally developed in the former Soviet Union. Former British Foreign Secretary Boris Johnson ranted that this required action by NATO, presumably characterizing it as an act of war. This sensational claim collapsed, however, when Porton Down, the British biological warfare lab, refused to back the major claim of the May government, and stated that it did not know from whence the nerve agent that poisoned the Skripals had come. The same conclusion was made by the international Organisation for the Prohibition of Chemical Weapons (OPCW). This seems abundantly clear, as the two now-dissident scientists who developed the agent now live in the United States, and published its formula all over the Internet. Further, both Skripal and his daughter survived the attack, pointing to far less competent putative assassins, and a far less potent agent than that proclaimed by the British government.

Once again, however, we find Christopher Steele in the middle of this new attack on Russia. Pablo Miller was Skripal's MI6 handler. He met with him regularly in Salisbury, and arranged speaking engagements for him in the former East Bloc countries. Not surprisingly, Miller is an associate at Steele's firm, Orbis Business Intelligence. Speculation is rife in British intelligence circles that Skripal played a role in the composing of the fake dirty dossier against Trump, and had become a liability to his controllers.

Given what we now know about Steele, and the dodgy, completely fake British intelligence dossier used to conduct a new British insurrection against the United States, why should the President tolerate the sanctions imposed by his State Department and manufactured by the same group of people who have tried to destroy him? It is really now time to take up LaRouche PAC's call, Mr. President: *End the Special Relationship and Declassify All British-Spawned Documents Concerning Your 2016 Campaign.* Fish really does stink from the head down.

The New Silk Road Gives a New Meaning To the Trans-European Network

by Ercole Incalza

Ercole Incalza was responsible for the General Transportation Plan approved by the Italian government in 1986, and updated in 1991. He has been active in the transport sector for thirty years, including being the CEO, for seven years, of Italy's high speed TAV (Treno Alta Velocità) rail service, and a key person in the creation of high-speed rail in Italy. After 2000, Incalza was involved in the European Union's TEN-T (Trans-European Transport Network), an integrated system of road, rail, air, and water networks on a European-wide scale. From 2008 to 2014, he was the head of the Italian government task force for carrying out its Strategic Infrastructure projects.

Mr. Incalza published the following report on his blog stanzediercole.com on Aug. 10 and authorized its reproduction in EIR. This is an edited translation.

Dagospia
Ercole Incalza

Aug. 11—To understand how the Mediterranean Basin has matured, over the last forty years—from being a geographic center of strategic importance into being a key economic area for the growth and development of a new system encompassing the whole planet—we need to carefully review the evolution of the programs and plans made beginning in 1985.

Italy, during its tenure as the rotating chairman of the European Union (EU) in 1985, proposed a Master Plan for the transport system of the entire EU commu-nity (at that time composed of only twelve states). The proposal was accepted and approved by the European Council. We review here the very interesting future directions for such systems proposed then, and the conclusions of this early programmatic tool. There were four project areas:

- Infrastructure corridors of common interest,
- Cross-border transit questions,
- Functional reorganization of different transport modalities, and
- Security issues.

In 1994, Henning Christophersen, then European Commissioner for Economic and Financial Affairs, made the first large-scale proposal consistent with Italy's proposed Master Plan, outlining the infrastructural priorities of the transport sector in the European Union and identifying nine Pan-European Corridors—multimodal road-railway infrastructure corridors that would connect the western and eastern parts of the European Union, the east being then an area which did not yet include EU members. Two of the proposed corridors would go through Italy—the Verona-Munich axis and the Trieste-Kiev axis. Christophersen's proposal clearly acknowledged that the Mediterranean was becoming more and more relevant to the growth and development in a new European Union. Beginning then, an organic planning process of the entire EU arrangement was initiated and it has, in fact, never stopped. In this regard, we cannot but remember EU Transport Commissioner Karel Van Miert's oft repeated words: "The European Union is similar to a very slow moving train which however never stops."

Certainly, the process that led to the current structure has been a long one and it has gone through two additional, distinct programmatic versions. The first was outlined in the 2004 TEN-T Networks document,

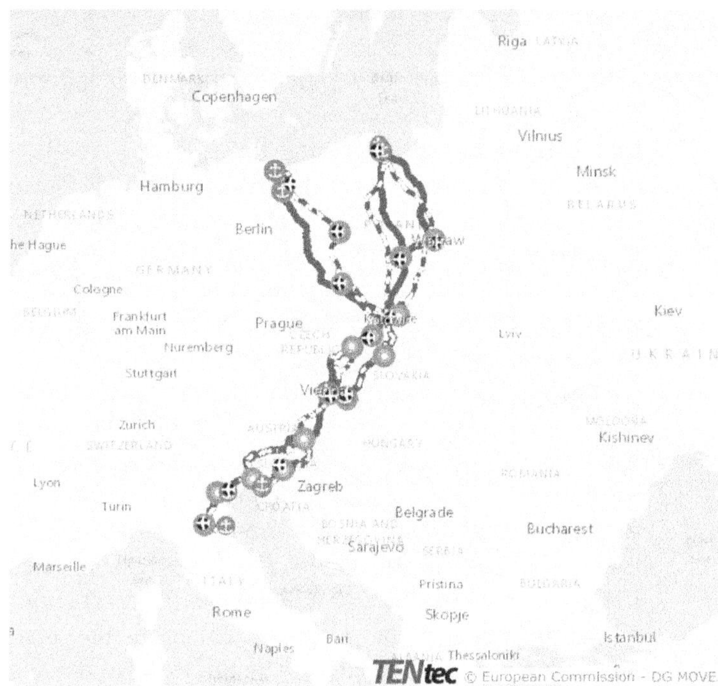

and the second in the 2012 TEN-T paper. The latter made the plan more effective with a greater, and well-motivated, strategic approach because it was not limited to the rail and road corridors, but also identified the metropolitan and logistic junctions (ports, airports, interports) of the entire EU system, a system which, by 2012, was composed of 28 countries.

The Mediterranean Basin is the common denominator of these programmatic and strategically focused steps and is the strong center of a large economic theater of action which, year after year, is becoming more important as the pivot between the economic systems of Europe and the African continent. It is important to note that the following four—of the nine EU Corridors as defined by the European Union's TEN-T Network 2012—run through the Mediterranean Basin region and Italy:

- **Baltic-Adriatic Corridor:** A multimodal North-South axis connecting the Baltic and Adriatic Seas, con-

necting key Italian and Polish ports and providing transportation links through Poland, the Czech Republic, Slovakia and Italy.

- **Mediterranean Corridor:** A Southern axis running from Algeciras in southern Spain through France and Northern Italy, to Hungary and Ukraine.

- **Scandinavian-Mediterranean Corridor:** A North-South land and sea axis going from the Baltic Sea, starting at the Finnish-Russian border, through Sweden to the European mainland and then to Germany and Italy, connecting to Malta through Sicily.

- **Rhine-Alpine Corridor:** A North-South infrastructural axis going through some of the most industrialized and heavily populated regions in Europe, going from Rotterdam and Antwerp on the North Sea to the Port of Genoa on the Mediterranean Sea.

A New Programmatic Idea

Strange as it may seem, the TEN-T Networks would have been limited in scope to a Europe-only scheme, remaining disconnected from the economies of the African and Asian continents, *were it not for a*

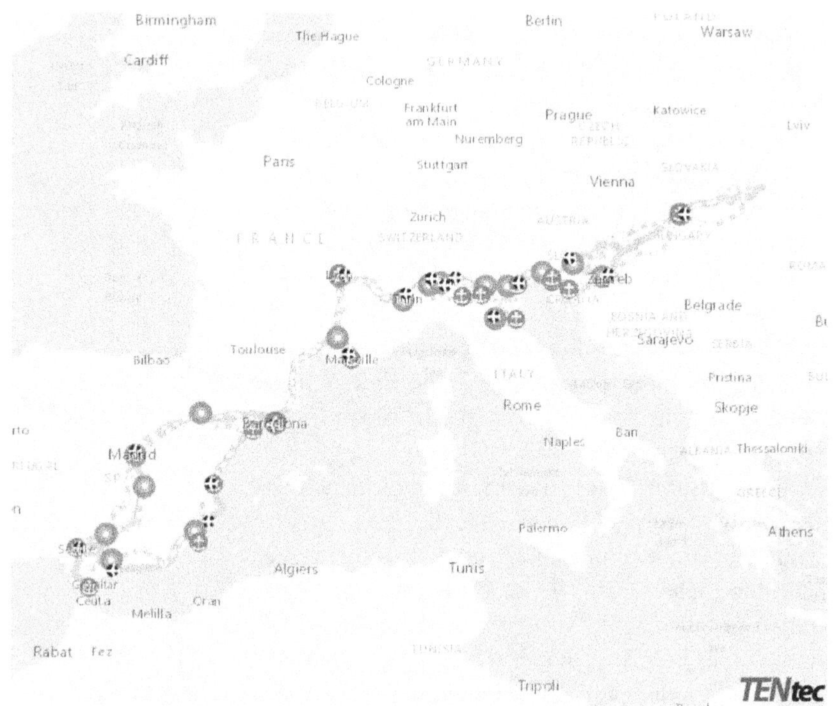

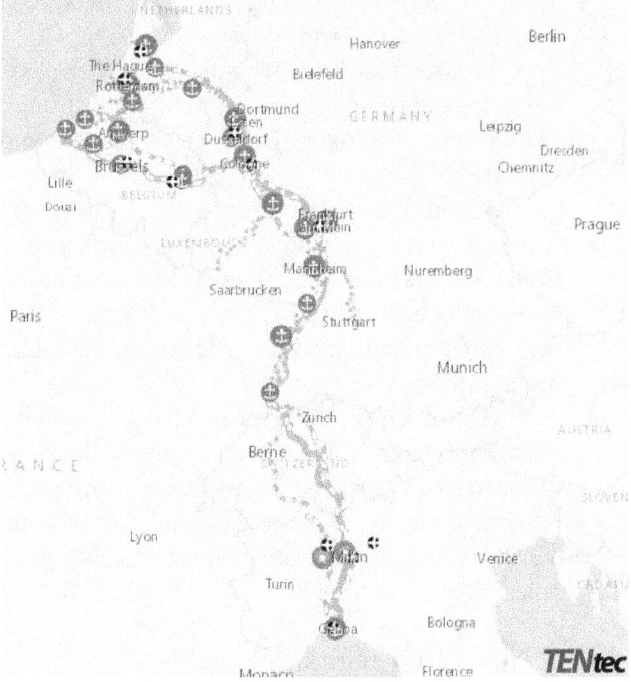

programmatic idea that arose and overcame every provincial or fractured local plan, every short-sighted passion for some particular logistical concern. That really revolutionary intervention was, and is, China's One Belt One Road, the New Silk Road, a project that is building an increasing interaction among Europe, Africa and Asia, and which, up to a few years ago, had not yet been linked by a functional logistics system.

The One Belt One Road initiative is not a banal declaration of intent. We have, with this extended project, an organic plan for land and sea connections. In fact, the "belt" component of the Belt and Road Initiative was publicly announced by Chinese President Xi Jinping in September 2013, and the "maritime road" component in October of the same year. At the same time, China put forward the proposal to create the Asian Infrastructure Investment Bank (AIIB) with a capital of $100 billion. This strategic evolution, which was really unthinkable just a decade ago, is an organic part of the evolutionary growth of the entire Mediterranean Basin, in which Italian ports can play a key role, and it urgently demands an act of intellectual humility: *We must therefore not only master this new language of logistics, but we must evaluate, in depth, all management approaches that for many years have proved inadequate for the needs of evolving demands.*

The new system is wiping out the old dichotomy between North Sea and Mediterranean ports, as well as the useless competition among Italy's own ports. It is creating new alternative connections between China and Europe and is creating a measurable competition between sea transport and land rail transport, using the latest technological generation of container ships (with capacities of up to 20,000 containers) as an instrument to optimize logistical processes.

Facing this new reality of the Mediterranean Basin, these new forms of approach to "logistics" through what we call the "supply chain"—the organic management of the entire production chain and the distribution of products—the approach of the current Italian government in reviewing some strategic choices, appears to be truly mediocre and provincial. Such a short-sightedness is so serious that it could irreversibly marginalize our country and alienate it from this epochal process of growth.

When, in our old ways, we finally understand how irresponsible such a choice was, will it not then be too late?

Scandinavian-Mediterranean

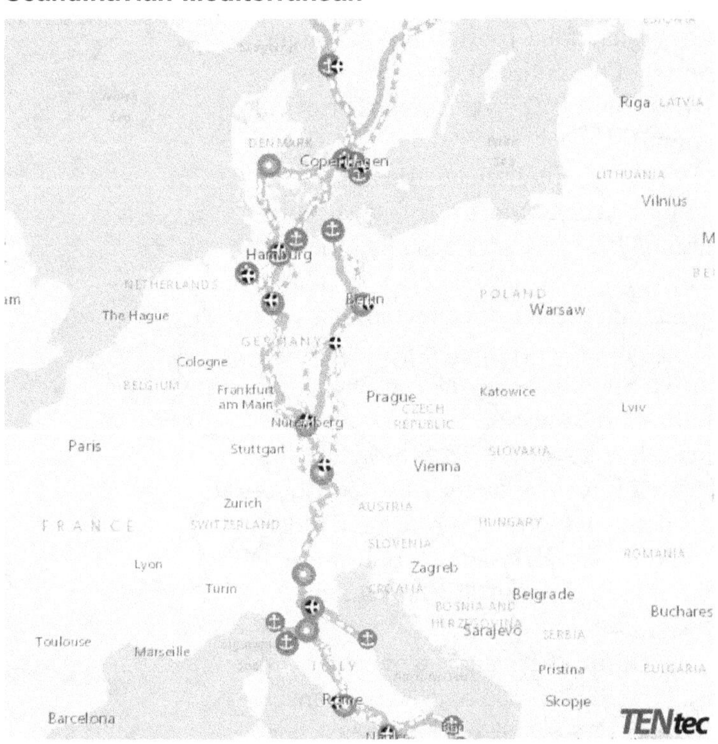

British Technology Strangled

by Mike Robinson

Mike Robinson is the Economics editor for the UK Column, *based in Plymouth, UK.*

PLYMOUTH, UK, Aug. 12—The post Second World War period was a golden opportunity for British engineering and manufacturing. Never in a position to compete with the sheer scale of output of the United States or Germany, Britain was nonetheless in a prime position to capitalize on the momentum of scientific and engineering development that had become necessary during the course of the war.

Yet in the decades that followed, successive governments withheld the funding necessary to fully realize Britain's engineering creativity and in some cases bargained it away, while at the same time, the British media did everything it could to ridicule British engineering efforts. As a result, British manufacturing has been decimated, and Britain turned into the City of London's vision of the post-industrial society.

Let's take a look at a few examples.

Britain's Space Program

Following the end of the Second World War, along with the United States and the Soviet Union, Britain was a serious contender in the race to develop rocket technology. Weapons delivery was initially the main driver, and for a while Britain's rocket program was the envy of the world.

Described as "perhaps the most economical and powerful space missile of its time," Britain's first iteration was called Black Knight. Between 1958 and

A Black Arrow launch vehicle, similar to the one that launched the UK's first satellite in 1971.

1965, Black Knight had managed 22 launches and reached an altitude of 500 miles.

Black Knight was originally developed to test designs for Britain's intermediate range ballistic missile program, called Blue Streak, which was intended to maintain Britain's independent nuclear deterrent capability. Blue Streak was cancelled before it became operational in its military role, but embarrassed by the wasted money, the British government decided to repurpose Blue Streak, along with parts of the Black Knight program, as a civilian satellite launch system called Black Prince.

Black Prince never actually got off the ground. Britain had already begun looking towards the European continent instead, and rather than funding Black Prince, decided to join the European Launcher Development Organization.

Britain's independent efforts did not end there, however. Another Black Knight derivative was called Black Arrow—a three-stage satellite carrier rocket, designed to be able to accept a fourth, Blue Streak–based stage, for larger payloads.

Black Arrow carried out four test launches between 1969 and 1971. The final launch carried the Prospero X-3 satellite into orbit. This was the first and only successful orbital launch carried out by the UK and took place three months following the sudden cancellation of the project. The only reason the launch took place at all was that the rocket had already been shipped to the launch site.

The launch site itself was scrapped as soon as the

launch was completed, and half of the scientists and engineers involved on the project lost their jobs. As we will see later, this was not the last time such an act of state sabotage would be carried out.

Black Knight, Blue Streak and Black Arrow represented world-beating British engineering. NASA was so threatened by Black Arrow, for example, that they offered Britain free satellite launches. As soon as Britain cancelled Black Arrow, the potential competition removed, NASA withdrew the offer.

Some have offered a compelling argument that the handing over of Britain's rocket technology to the European Launcher Development Organization and the eventual sudden cancellation of Black Arrow was part of negotiations by Britain to join the EEC (the embryonic European Union).

To date, Britain is the only country to have ever successfully developed and then abandoned a satellite launch capability.

CC/Sandman5

A BAC TSR-2 tactical strike/reconnaissance jet.

The Canberra and the TSR-2

Another area where Britain was at the forefront of post-war technological development was aviation. Britain's first jet bomber, the English Electric Canberra, was more capable than any aircraft in its class, setting a world record altitude of over 70,000 feet. It was a commercial success, including 400 built under license in the United States.

However, as the Soviet Union developed its surface-to-air missile capabilities, the Canberra and other high-altitude type aircraft became vulnerable to attack. The Ministry of Supply in Britain decided a new light bomber was needed to replace the Canberra.

The timing of the decision could not have been worse. Wartime aircraft procurement had been a matter of competition between well over a dozen separate companies. As successful as this was while wartime budgets existed, the British government made it clear that the contract for the new light bomber would only be awarded to companies willing to collaborate.

In parallel, political pressure was beginning to build against the very idea of manned aircraft. Duncan Sandys, then Minister of Defense, published a White Paper in which he claimed that the era of ballistic missiles had arrived, and in addition, he argued, a missile program would offer significant cost savings over manned aircraft.

Despite the political infighting between government and military top brass caused by the Sandys White Paper, the go-ahead was given in 1959 to produce a design for a new light bomber which would again be a world-beater.

The new aircraft, named TSR-2 (tactical strike/reconnaissance), was to be capable of takeoff from just 600 yards of runway, of Mach 1.1 at 600 feet, and Mach 2.2 at high altitude. The final design exceeded these requirements, with a theoretical maximum speed of Mach 3 at 45,000 feet.

As design morphed into production, however, it became clear that the original cost estimates were vastly underestimated. Development problems with engines and undercarriage were leapt upon as political footballs, not least by a press determined to undermine British innovation. While test pilots reported outstanding basic flight capabilities, with the aircraft achieving Mach 1.12 at 200 feet, the press reported spiraling costs and technical difficulties, and promoted the U.S. rival, the F-111.

A British Airways Concorde. This time, the press had the "Anti-Concorde Project," led by environmental activist Richard Wiggs and backed up by academics from Cambridge University and University College London, feeding it all the propaganda it could want.

In 1965, British Defense Secretary Dennis Healey suddenly cancelled the project. In another act of state sabotage, all machine tooling and jigs were immediately scrapped, as were any airframes in production. Three of these suffered an ignominious end as "damage to aircraft" targets at Shoeburyness shooting range. Two airframes survived and became museum pieces, as did the British aviation industry.

Aeronautical engineer Sir Sydney Camm, designer of the World War II Hawker Hurricane fighter, said of the TSR-2: "All modern aircraft have four dimensions: span, length, height and politics. TSR-2 simply got the first three right."

TSR-2 is remembered as the aircraft shot down by its own government, with the unwavering complicity of the press.

The Concorde

The only major British aeronautical project to survive the cancellations resulting from the TSR-2 fiasco was Concorde, a supersonic passenger jet, capable of flying a regular scheduled service at over 1,300 miles per hour. A joint venture between the newly formed British Aircraft Corporation and France's Aerospatiale, Concorde used a unique wing design, a fly-by-wire control system, thrust-by-wire engine control systems and computer controlled engine intakes—all pioneering technologies.

Development began in the early 1950s. By the end of the decade it became apparent that the French were pursuing a similar program and that they had, in fact, come up with similar design solutions to the main technical problems of supersonic flight. It was decided, therefore, that the project should proceed as a joint Anglo-French effort. A treaty was signed, a name given and development began in earnest.

Once again, though, as construction and testing of the first two prototypes progressed, including its first public outing at the Paris airshow in 1969, the British press stepped in to ensure the project was a failure.

Following the airshow appearance, both aircraft began a world sales and demonstration tour with a view to winning orders from the United States and the Far East, to a barrage of press negativity. This time, the press had the "Anti-Concorde Project," led by environmental activist Richard Wiggs and backed up by academics from Cambridge University and University College London, feeding it all the propaganda it could want.

Just as today, the press simply uncritically regurgitated what they were fed. "Supersonic Bust" and a host of other headlines brought fear of sonic booms, dirty exhausts and noisy take-offs to the gullible public, in the process scuppering any opportunity for export sales as foreign airlines shied away from the bad publicity.

The media never let up with the anti-Concorde publicity. As recently as 2001, when flights had been suspended following its only fatal accident, a headline in the *Independent* newspaper read "Concorde—noisy and dirty, and we can live without it."

"But just because we can do something with the technology we have developed," they wrote, "does not mean that we have to do it all the time. We managed to fly men to the Moon and back in 1969; yet somehow we have resisted the enormous temptation to have weekly passenger cruises out there. Concorde pollutes the atmosphere and isn't necessary. We haven't missed it. Let's do without it."

We should not have done without it. Concorde represented the cutting edge of British engineering in its industry sector. It was an inspiration to future engineers and loved by the public.

At the end of the day, it was a commercial success for the airlines that bought it, yet negative press coverage guaranteed a "supersonic bust" for the manufacturers; the only airlines to buy it were British Airways and Air France.

public domain

The Advanced Passenger Train. Progress on the development of the Advanced Passenger Train continued to stall, with the broader management and funding issues suffered by British Rail filtering down to the project team.

The Advanced Passenger Train

Britain has led the way in the development of rail transport since the 18th Century. By the middle of the 20th, though, things were changing.

Britain's railways had been nationalized following World War II. Finances became rapidly poorer over the subsequent decade. The so-called Beeching reforms saw the closure of 7,000 miles of railways between 1950 and 1973, significantly higher than the 5,000 miles and 2,363 stations envisaged by Dr Richard Beeching's original report. He would not have objected.

Nonetheless, British Rail continued to innovate. A team of engineers began work in the 1960s to build an Advanced Passenger Train (APT) which would be capable of speeds of at least 125 miles per hour, and would include the ability to "tilt" round corners, allowing faster cornering speeds without the need to lay new track.

The ability to tilt was not the only innovation on the APT. Its braking system used a combination of hydrokinetic braking in concert with traditional braking systems, air conditioning throughout the train, and power-operated doors.

By the end of the 1960s it was becoming apparent that the APT was not progressing quickly enough, mainly because of underfunding, and so effort was diverted into an interim project to get high-speed trains into operation while work on the more advanced APT technologies continued.

The first prototype of what was to become the InterCity 125 was completed in the summer of 1972. During tests in the autumn of that year, it reached speeds of 143.2 miles per hour.

The first-production InterCity went into operation in 1975, and these trains are still running today, with a replacement program only beginning last month.

In the meantime, progress on the development of the Advanced Passenger Train continued to stall, with the broader management and funding issues suffered by British Rail filtering down to the project team.

By 1981 Margaret Thatcher was two years into her first term as Prime Minister, and threatened to cancel the project. British Rail management thought that a sensible response to this problem would be to get the APT prototypes into service. So, to great fanfare, a train packed with journalists began its inaugural round trip between Glasgow and London.

The southbound leg was huge success, setting a speed record of 4 hours 14 minutes to cover the 401 mile journey.

However, on the return trip, the lack of redundancy in some of the systems installed on the prototypes became painfully apparent, resulting in the failure of the tilting mechanism, "sending food across tables, spilling drinks and jamming the electronic doors." The media immediately begin their campaign to discredit the project, with monikers such as "queasy rider." Rather than celebrating the technical innovation and the speed record, every problem with the prototype, large or small, was given full media treatment. The project never recovered.

Four years later, with no fanfare, the three prototype APTs quietly began operations on the same route once again, this time successfully. However, the Inter-City 125 had by this time cornered the market. As with Concorde, media coverage of APT had guaranteed that it could not be sold in export markets. Plans for production trains were abandoned.

One year later, the three APTs was taken out of service and scrapped. The patents for the APT tilting mechanism were sold to FIAT in Italy.

The total amount of money spent on APT over its 15-year lifespan was £50 million. The TGV (Très Grande Vitesse) in France cost twenty times as much to get into service.

In 2001, the APT's tilting technology returned to the London-Glasgow route, when Richard Branson's Virgin Trains brought in 57 Italian Pendolino trains which finally beat APT's southbound speed record in 2006, completing the journey from Glasgow to London in 3 hours 55 minutes. APT still holds the outright speed record, having completed a run from London to Glasgow in 3 hours 54 minutes in 1984, which included a five-minute delay because of a signal failure.

The Future

How, then, are things looking for the future? Sadly, the same behavior by the government and mainstream media applies to Britain's latest high-speed rail project, HS2 (High Speed 2), which is planned to link London with the northern English cities of Manchester and Leeds.

The HS2 route map. The HS2 project has experienced exactly the same type of government sabotage and media coverage as the Advanced Passenger Train, the TSR2, and the Concorde.

With a top design speed of 250 mph, unlikely to be achieved in practice, HS2 is hardly at the cutting edge of railway technology. It's not really a British project, either, with the contracts for engines and rolling stock likely to go to foreign companies. In fact, the Department for Transport's design recommendations used an image of the French AGV (Automotrice Grande Vitesse) train as a suitable example. It will, nonetheless, finally bring British intercity rail up to the standard France has enjoyed since the early 1980s, if it manages to get into operation.

Nonetheless, the HS2 project has experienced exactly the same type of government sabotage and media coverage as the Advanced Passenger Train, TSR2 and Concorde. Headlines such as "The HS2 rail project is out of date and out of control. But it can still be halted"; "HS2 'gravy train' slammed as 1 in 4 staff paid more than £100,000 of taxpayer's cash"; and "HS2: a scheme bound to go off the rails" are just three headlines from one recent media day. The media pressure has been incessant since the project was announced in 2009.

For seventy years, successive British governments of all political persuasions have systematically undermined British industry and innovation. I have highlighted several specific projects in this article, but the same patterns of behavior by government and media can be seen with respect to the British steel, coal, shipbuilding, and car industries.

Throughout its history, Britain has demonstrated that it is able to produce world class innovators and engineers. What positive contribution could they make if British policy would permit them to express their capabilities unhindered?

Contact the author at: mike@ukcolumn.org

The Time Has Come To End the Russiagate Fraud!

This is the edited transcript of the August 10, 2018 Schiller Institute New Paradigm webcast, an interview with the founder of the Schiller Institutes, Helga Zepp-LaRouche. She was interviewed by Harley Schlanger. A video *of the webcast is available.*

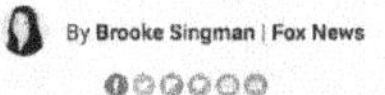

Senior Justice Department official Bruce Ohr, left, continued to communicate with former British spy Christopher Steele, right, even after the FBI cut ties with him. (AP)

Harley Schlanger: Hello! I'm Harley Schlanger from the Schiller Institute. I welcome you to this week's strategic briefing from founder of the Schiller Institutes, Helga Zepp-LaRouche.

In the past few weeks, we're seeing growing battles, battles that are going to shape the future of the world. There are the tremendous potentials associated with the Belt and Road Initiative, with what we've called the Singapore spirit, and the optimism of the Trump-Putin Helsinki Summit. But we're also seeing a really grinding battle in the United States over Russiagate, which took a new turn this week when President Trump's attorney, Rudy Giuliani, very combatively attacked the entire Mueller operation, saying that this is going to be turned upside-down; it's going to blow up against the accusers. We're now seeing more revelations about the role of Christopher Steele and his British MI6 connections. So Helga, why don't we start there? Incredible battles are taking place now, in the background, around Russiagate.

Russiagate: A British Intelligence Operation

Helga Zepp-LaRouche: I would say that the atmosphere in the United States has become so hysterical that one has the feeling of a showdown between the forces of the British Empire—the collusion between the Obama-administration heads of U.S. intelligence agencies with British intelligence—and Trump. This is escalating. There is a clear perception in the rest of the world, in Russia, in China, and even in North Korea.

People there are making a very clear distinction between policies coming from President Trump and policies which come from high officials in his administration. The attacks are obviously designed to prevent Trump from pursuing his North Korea policy, and his policy with President Putin and Russia, and at the same time to promote escalating antagonism against China. All of this is extremely dangerous.

I think the only way to defeat those attacks is to do exactly what our colleagues in the United States have just done in publishing a new report, "Fish Stinks from the Head" I urge all our viewers, to get this report. Download it, read it, discuss it, and get it around as far as possible, because it documents exactly what is wrong with this apparatus. Not only did Giuliani say that this thing would blow up big, but also that it is not about Trump—it's what *they* did. They, here, is the combination of the Obama intelligence people with the British. This will lead to a completely new Watergate and reform. But there is no guaranteed outcome. This is an ongoing British intelligence operation that is now being made more and more public.

The Hill newspaper in Washington had an article two days ago, reporting that Christopher Steele, who was fired by the FBI in November 2016 for leaking information to the media, subsequently had about 60 meetings with Bruce Ohr, then Deputy Attorney General. In an exchange of texts in August 2017, Steele offered to rejoin Special Counsel Robert Mueller's operation to help speed up Mueller's investigation. Rod Rosenstein, the present Deputy Attorney General, claimed that he did not know what Bruce Ohr had been doing during those 60 meetings with Christopher Steele. This is disgraceful misconduct, and it is all described in "Fish Stinks from the Head."

I think the most important thing one can do to defend the Presidency against this coup attempt is to get this information in circulation as widely as possible. This is the battle of the century for mankind, because everything is heating up before the U.S. mid-term elections. Were the Democrats to win control of the House of Representatives, their first step would be to close down all Congressional investigations now occurring. Congressmen Bob Goodlatte and Trey Gowdy have just announced that they will subpoena everybody who has anything to do with the Christopher Steele operation this week.

That could turn the tide completely. I think the more people demand just such actions, and say things like Giuliani, the better the chances are of combatting the hysteria being created.

Gage Skidmore

Rudy Giuliani, former New York City Mayor.

Should the Democrats take control of the House, they would not only close down the investigations, but they would immediately go for impeachment, which could eventually restore the same apparatus that was there with Obama and Hillary. An unstoppable confrontation with Russia and China might then commence. So, there is really a lot at stake. I appeal to everyone listening: Mobilize and work with us to circulate the article as widely as possible.

Schlanger: This new article, "Fish Stinks from the Head," is written by Barbara Boyd, who also wrote the original article on Mueller and his role going back to the 1980s in the "Get LaRouche" taskforce. This article, and its mass circulation, is just the latest example of the work we have been doing to expose the British connections—Richard Dearlove, Steele, and the penetration by this network of the Trump campaign through Brennan, Clapper, and Comey, among others.

Our organizing and publishing has been instrumental in getting Congress to act. I would add that the FISA warrant that Rep. Devin Nunes is still trying to get declassified is quite significant. Now there's a push to get Trump, as Giuliani said, to declassify all the documents. We had called for the declassification of every document that had a connection to British intelligence. To reiterate your point Helga, if the British connection gets out, it can blow the whole thing up.

You mentioned the mid-term elections. What can, and should, be done? There are big problems in the Republican Party, including foreign policy toward Russia and China. Maybe we should go to that. What do you make of all these sanctions? This is part of the same battle, isn't it?

CC/International Education Foundation

Rod Rosenstein, Deputy Attorney General.

Whither U.S. Foreign Policy?

Zepp-LaRouche: This problem comes from the neo-con element in the Trump administration. Just when Trump tries to get a decent relationship going with Russia, Trump is prevailed upon to impose new sanctions because of the so-called Skripal affair, for which there is, in fact, zero evidence. I think the Russian Foreign Ministry, on the contrary, provided a lot of information on the work of the British Empire and British intelligence. There has been zero proof that Russia was involved in the Skripal poisonings. The Russians are reacting to these new sanctions, which potentially target Russian banking internationally, quite a severe escalation. Prime Minister Medvedev reacted extremely sharply, saying that Russia has to regard the sanctions as a declaration of economic warfare, that Russia will have to take appropriate countermeasures, and that this could have unforeseeable consequences.

I think this is really playing with fire. Russia could go out of the dollar, and go for a completely different kind of financial system, which is one of the many mines which could blow up the entire system. This is really dangerous stuff. Look at the avalanche of sanctions—new sanctions against North Korea, despite the indications that North Korea is doing everything agreed upon between Trump and Kim; new sanctions against Iran; new sanctions against Turkey, over a detained American pastor—a measure completely out of proportion that can only drive Turkey further away from the West and into the dynamic of the BRICS. President Erdogan has already announced, in the context of the Johannesburg BRICS Summit, that Turkey wants to become a member of the BRICS and the BRICS should be called BRICST, with the T at the end for Turkey.

If someone wants to blow up the financial system and blow up NATO, then these actions driving Russia off dollar-denominated international commerce and driving Turkey into the BRICS may be precisely the right thing to do. I think these are very dangerous developments. In a lengthy interview with RT—regarded by some as the devil, but just a news organ, former U.S. diplomat Jim Jatras pointed to the fact that all these sanctions are just one step removed from breaking diplomatic relations and going to war. Indeed, if you look at the anti-Russia hysteria, and now a growing xenophobia, which the Chinese media have picked

Xinhua

Recep Tayyip Erdogan, President of Turkey.

up on very clearly, I think this is very unhealthy. It's crazy. In what world do these people think they live? What do they want to do to resolve this? Regime change in Russia, in China, in Iran? The only way to counter this is to say that if the United States wants to solve the economic problems, if an uncontrolled financial blow-out of the entire financial system is to be avoided, we need a Four-Power Agreement to create a New Bretton Woods system and implement the Four Laws of Lyndon LaRouche. For that to be successful, you cannot antagonize the very countries you need to make the kind of reforms which are a lifesaver for the whole civilization.

I urge, you, our audience, not to fall into this anti-Russia, anti-China hysteria, because it can only lead to a catastrophe. What we need instead is win-win cooperation with these countries. There is a lot of reason to be worried about achieving that cooperation, because even some of Trump's supporters and some Congressmen who support Trump and who are working against the British coup, fall for the propaganda against Russia and China. In my view, this is based on very little knowledge about what these countries actually stand for. Again, I urge you not to fall into this hysteria, but to work with us for a New Bretton Woods system.

Dissent Disallowed

Schlanger: Just two additional notes on the anti-Russia sanctions. When it was announced two days ago that these new sanctions were being implemented by the U.S. government over the Skripal affair, Trump said nothing about it. The media and others were critical of Trump for not taking the lead in pushing this.

I think the other thing that's important is a new Senate bill being worked on by the usual suspects—Lindsey Graham, John McCain, and Ben Cardin (who was very much involved in the Magnitsky Act). They are talking about new sanctions in response to allegations that Russia is preparing to intervene in the U.S. mid-term elections.

Now, this brings into view another facet of xenophobia. While polling shows that a healthy portion of the American population—in some cases 50%-60%—want discussions to go on with Russia, and they support Trump's meeting with Putin, we're now also witnessing the emergence of a much more aggressive thought police in the United States, attacking voices on the Internet and otherwise that speak out against the coup and in favor of the President. I wonder, Helga, if you have some thoughts on this Orwellian suppression of free speech?

Zepp-LaRouche: This is quite something, because it was the Atlantic Council that many months ago signed an agreement with YouTube to fish out all fake news, identifying it as Russian propaganda. So, when YouTube and Apple and some others closed down not only Alex Jones, but also an author from antiwar.com, from the Rand Paul Institute, this is all directed against,— Alex Jones for example, attacked Robert Mueller just before the shutdown occurred. Alex Jones has had 10 million viewers every month. In the last four weeks, he had 17 million viewers, 2.4 million on his YouTube channel.

This *is* a thought control. I can only hope that enough Americans will counter that and help to undo it. What kind of America will it be if there is only the official opinion—for example, that Russia was responsible for Trump's victory in the 2016 election, or man-made climate change? There's a whole series of formulas and dogmatic beliefs you have to have, but if you have a question, or maybe a different scientific opinion, well, you'd better get right with Big Brother.

The fact of the matter is that there are many scien-

tists who have completely different views on why Earth's climate changes, who look at climate from the standpoint of long-term cycles of the placement of the Solar system in our Galaxy, over millions and hundreds of millions of years, who point out that there has always been a cycle of ice ages, warming periods, small ice ages. The idea that it's all due to CO_2 emissions is questioned by many very serious scientists who have also proven that the way the statistics are being used is completely manipulated.

If you can't have a scientific debate, then it's the end of human creativity. This is worse than Goebbels; this is worse than the Stalin period. Where is democracy? Where is freedom of thought? YouTube and these other firms claim that they're not bound by the First Amendment because they're private corporations. This was the same argument, by the way, used by the Democratic Party against my husband in the election process, despite the fact that he had sufficient votes and delegates as a candidate, to be able to address the Democratic Party nominating convention. Then, the argument was that the Democratic Party is a private club!

When the people who hold up the banner of democracy and human rights and all of these—look at what they're doing! They're banning dissent! This is the thought police. This is absolutely Orwellian, and if this is not being fought but instead people submit to it, we are witnessing it the end of free America. People should really not let that happen.

Schlanger: Another way thought control occurs is

by keeping the American people completely ignorant of what you, Helga, been focussed on for the last two decades, really, which is the global movement for the Belt and Road Initiative, the World Land-Bridge, and so on. There's quite a bit going on with that, following the BRICS Summit in Johannesburg South Africa.

World Is Larger than Dreamed by Geopoliticians

Zepp-LaRouche: It's almost that you have two universes. Because of the leadership of the BRICS—especially China, but also Russia—there is a change in the dynamic on the African continent, there is a new motion forward.

I think we mentioned this already, but it's really important to reiterate: Because of the New Silk Road Spirit, the idea that you replace geopolitical confrontation with a "win-win cooperation" for joint ventures, for joint economic infrastructure projects, for joint science cooperation, and cultural exchanges, you have right now a changed political climate where, for example, there is a realistic chance, for the first time since Partition in 1947, that the conflict between India and Pakistan can be settled; you have a very exciting dynamic among the different countries of the Horn of Africa. Somalia, Djibouti, Eritrea, and Ethiopia have all started diplomatic relations with each other, and this is due to the Chinese railroad building between Djibouti and Addis Abeba. For the first time, there is economic development and hope. And this is also going on in many other African countries.

I made the point last week that more dangerous than fake news is the censorship by the mainstream media in not reporting on these positive developments. I made the reference to the 1920s and 1930s in Germany, when, because of the Versailles Treaty, because of the Great Depression, unemployment, right/left confrontations, because of World War II, people fell into a complete cultural pessimism. They were unrooted, they didn't see any options for the future, and this is why the Nazis could take power.

I made the point that there is a widespread cultural pessimism today in many of the Western countries, including in the United States. Life-expectancy, the clearest economic parameter if an economy is doing well or not, is *going down*. You now have this unbelievable drug epidemic—so many people have a hard time seeing any potential for a positive change for their lives in the future.

Trump promised that he would bring such a change, and hopefully he is doing this; he has done incredible things already, considering the opposition he's up against. In Germany, the mainstream media also do not report about the positive things happening in the developing nations. Most Germans think there's nothing that can be done anyway, and so they are falling again into mass cultural pessimism. This is very dangerous. Were people to see the chance for development of Africa, for the reconstruction of Southwest Asia, well, then, young people would want to become engineers, teachers, doctors, scientists. They would, once again, have hope. But when they only hear in the mainstream media negative news and no vision for the future, then the danger is that they will fall into cultural pessimism and go for really bad options.

I think this is something to be aware of. I encourage people: If YouTube is shutting down certain speakers, you still have the possibility to go to Internet sites of African nations, of Latin American nations, of Russia, China, and make your own judgment: Do not go by what they try to serve you. If you know what to look for, that there is a new world economic order emerging, then you can also verify it yourself—it takes a little bit of work. And, you should help us to spread this webcast, because we're trying to address the issues which are not being addressed otherwise.

Help us get this webcast known among your friends and colleagues and relatives. Let's work together against the efforts of the fake news to keep the people in Europe and the United States in the "Valley of the Clueless." That was the formulation used to describe the people in Dresden during the time of the German Democratic Republic (East Germany). People in East Germany would always listen to West German TV and radio, but because Dresden was situated in a valley, its people couldn't tune in to these broadcasts, and therefore were called the people in the "Valley of the Clueless."

And that is the condition of many Americans and Europeans now, because listening only to the mainstream media provides no chance, or almost no chance, to get a realistic picture of what the world really looks like.

Space Force vs. the Power of Great Ideas

Schlanger: A lot of what you're describing is the ongoing fight between the emerging New Paradigm and the desperate attempt to hold onto the old paradigm.

One area where this fight is clear is in space, where you have an enormous potential—African countries linking up with China; the Russians working with countries, Vietnam, India.

And yet, the idea of a Space Force, a new, sixth military command, concerned with and operating in outer space, was put forward yesterday in the United States, which is being portrayed as a "war against Russia and China." Is that how the Russians and the Chinese see this announcement by Vice President Pence?

Zepp-LaRouche: Yes. I think especially the Chinese responded very strongly. I'm sure there will be some Russian statements coming as well. What the Chinese basically said, was that militarizing space is completely unacceptable, that it was clear to all the nations so far that space is to be a peaceful place, and that this reflects an effort by the United States to control the world, to have hegemony over the world.

DoD/Vernon Young, Jr.

Vice President Mike Pence announces the creation of the U.S. Space Force to service members during a briefing at the Pentagon, Aug. 9, 2018.

Now, this must not be the last word. During the late 1970s and early 1980s, when you had the intermediate-range missile crisis between the Soviet SS-20s and the U.S. Pershing 2s, my husband developed a program which was later called the Strategic Defense Initiative, to make sure that in that time, the United States and the Soviet Union would work together to make nuclear weapons obsolete, through cooperation in space.

That potential still exists, but requires a slightly different approach. In any case, it was admitted that the Space Force is not effective against the Kinzhal, Russia's new hypersonic missile

So there is an incredible tension right now, between those forces who still want to stick to the unipolar world, a world which *de facto* no longer exists. As I have said many times, the dynamic expressed with the BRICS and the Global South countries working together to overcome underdevelopment, is in my view unstoppable, except by World War III. I mean, blowing up civilization settles that matter. But nobody would be the winner, including those who push such a crazy policy.

It is still possible to overcome all of the tensions by finding a solution on a higher level, a New Paradigm, win-win cooperation. But it will require that the United States clearly accept the fact of this new dynamic, and that even if you want to destroy it, you cannot.

Just take the fact that China has been the leading nation of the world for many centuries, and all it is doing right now is saying that it wants to have, again, a status as a world leader, with great power relationships which makes it an equal partner of the United States and others, and that China does not want to replicate the U.S. hegemonic model. If you take India and China together, the two most population-rich countries in the world, they have together 2.6 billion people. India also is on a very ambitious path, to cooperate with China now in Africa. Japan, too, wants to work with China to develop Africa.

If you think you can stop that, I think you are completely absurd and are operating with outmoded thinking. Looking at the long arc of history, when mankind finally controls and deploys thermonuclear fusion, mankind will have security in raw materials and energy for practically the indefinite future. We are at a major branching point in our history. However, if we try to stick to the status quo, which is already not defendable any more, it can only lead to a disaster.

What we need is a new thinking. I have always called it the thinking of the "coincidence of opposites," the higher level of the one humanity, what Xi Jinping calls the "community of a shared future for mankind."

We need this kind of new thinking, the total counter to the present anti-Russia and anti-China hysteria. Once again, if you are not already doing so, I urge you to start thinking this way, because it's the human way. We are one human species. The astronauts always say, if you look from a space station down to the Earth, you see the one humanity and you see how fragile our little blue planet is, and you don't think in terms of world war and geopolitical control; you think about what you can do to make sure the Earth is not hit by a meteor. One hit Greenland the other day—another reminder that we had better concentrate on these common aims of mankind.

Help us stem this tide of thought police and crazy efforts by geopoliticians to go for confrontation. Let's have a different approach: Diplomatic solutions are always possible, dialogue. There is no problem on this planet which cannot be solved through dialogue and diplomacy. War must never again be a means of political conflict resolution. Clausewitz is dead.

Schlanger: [laughs] Well, two things you can do immediately after watching this webcast: 1. Join the Schiller Institute, to become part of the group of thinkers that is changing the world, and 2. Order your own copy of *The New Silk Road Becomes the World Land-Bridge, Vol. II*, to give you the details that you need so that you can be a thoughtful leader of people around you, to help them also understand exactly this New Paradigm.

Helga, we've covered a lot. Is there anything else you want to add?

Zepp-LaRouche: I want all of you to become more active—this is showdown time. If things go wrong, we could be *really* in a terrible crisis, much worse than it is now. However, if we defeat this coup, then the United States will be a very beautiful place.

NEW RELEASE, **Volume II**

The New Silk Road Becomes the World Land-Bridge:

A Shared Future For Humanity

The spirit of the New Silk Road is changing the world for the better. The exciting overview in this new 440-page Volume II report updates the roadmap given in Volume I, on the coming into being of the World Land-Bridge for development and peace. BRICS countries have a strategy to prevent war and economic catastrophe. It's time for the rest of the world to join!

Includes:

Introduction by Helga Zepp-LaRouche, "A Shared Future for Humanity."

Progress Reports on development corridors worldwide, spurred by China's Belt and Road Initiative. Features 140 maps.

Principles of Physical Economy by Lyndon LaRouche, especially his "Four Laws" for emergency action in the Trans-Atlantic.

Soft cover (440 pages)
Domestic Price: $60. Shipping cost included in price.
Foreign Price: $60. Add $15 per copy for shipping.
Order from **newparadigm.schillerinstitute.com**
Tel 1 703 297 8368

Giuseppe Castiglione (1688-1766), Jesuit Painter in the Forbidden City: Unifying Spirit Between East and West

by Matthew Ehret-Kump

This report is written in honor of Helga Zepp-La-Rouche, who has dedicated her life to bringing out the best in every culture, on her 70th Birthday.

In pursuing the Belt and Road Initiative, we should ensure that when it comes to different civilizations, exchange will replace estrangement, mutual learning will replace clashes, and coexistence will replace a sense of superiority. This will boost mutual understanding, mutual respect and mutual trust among different countries.

> —Xi Jinping, Belt and Road Summit, 2017

Now that a new paradigm of trust, mutual respect and cooperation amongst the various cultures of the world has taken on a new empowering life, led by Xi Jinping's vision of the Belt and Road Initiative, the Shanghai Cooperation Organization and the BRICS, thinking citizens must take the opportunity now to embody the best character of this new renaissance spirit.

This means that instead of looking only at what separates the various cultures of the world as distinct from their neighbors, the time has come to commit ourselves to a true universal renaissance, whereby each culture finds what is most beautiful, good and truthful in itself and also in its neighbors. The best discoveries of each culture, when cross-pollinated in this way, will create a new and incredible "one" that will always be more than the sum of its parts, and will contain a greater degree of potential for creative expression and understanding than each could sustain on its own.

A Renaissance Mind in the Forbidden City

For those not familiar with the figure of Giuseppe Castiglione (also known as Lang Shi Ning, 1688-1766), it is extremely rewarding to explore his works and incredible life as the court painter of three emperors of China during the Qing Dynasty (Kangxi, Yongzhen and Qianlong) from 1715 to his death in Beijing in 1766.

Although very little today remains of Castiglione's original letters and writings, his genius can still be strikingly felt and studied. Born in Milan and trained in the renowned Botheghe degli Stanpator art studio by master painters Carlo Cornara and Andrea Pozzo, Castiglione was contracted to produce paintings for Jesuit churches in Italy before he headed off to China at the age of 19. Emperor Kangxi had requested the services of Jesuit specialists in optical perspective, painting, mechanics, clock making, medicine, enameling and topographical projections.

Giuseppe Castiglione with scientific instruments introduced into China by the Jesuits.

Castiglione's style harmonically blended the most powerful discoveries of the West with the East, including linear perspective, chiaroscuro (albeit in an extremely subdued form to satisfy Chinese aesthetic tastes), and refined Chinese pigments and poetic symbolism. Although missionary painters had been trying since the time of Matteo Ricci (1552-1610) to introduce western artistic styles into China, painting never found an organic form to take hold until Castiglione.[1]

His use of oil techniques, combining renaissance realism with Chinese pigments and styles, had never been accomplished in an organic manner before. His style became known as Xianfa or "line method," a technique which, while beautiful, was incredibly challenging, as the tempera-on-silk process was much more unforgiving for mistakes compared to traditional canvases used in Europe. Castiglione not only revolutionized painting but also copperplate engravings, architecture, and even enameling, crafting new techniques and blending styles in eastern and western aesthetics in all domains.[2]

Upon arriving in China, Castiglione was immediately called to the Imperial Court and asked to paint a bird for Emperor Kangxi who was so impressed with the young man's work that he soon assigned him ten students.

Emperor Kangxi (1661-1722) had been educated both by the official Confucian scholars and by the Jesuit missionaries in the Court. He became a close collaborator with the Jesuits in the study of astronomy, science, music, and philosophy. He believed firmly in the coherence of the Christian teachings of the Jesuit

Castiglione's "Bean Flowers and Millet."

Matteo Ricci

Fathers and the core philosophic outlook of the Confucian tradition in China, and had issued an edict to allow the Jesuits to proselytize freely throughout the country.

Like Matteo Ricci, who had first established the cooperation between the Jesuit Fathers and the Court during his time in China (from 1583 until his death in 1610), and also like Emperor Kangxi, Castiglione believed in uniting and transforming both Chinese and European cultures through a pursuit of beauty and excellence in all domains of science, the arts, and engineering. It was recognized by these great thinkers that simply preaching a religious text was not sufficient to do justice to God's will, and that nothing short of studying the book of nature in pursuit of the mind of God would suffice at truly winning converts and allies.

Sadly, none of Castiglione's works from the period in Kangxi's Court have survived. The earliest surviving works by Castiglione begin in the reign of Kangxi's son, Emperor Yongzheng (1722-1735). These include the 1723 hanging scroll, "Gathering of Auspicious Signs" [**Figure 1**], produced for the new emperor's inauguration, and his famous "One Hundred Steeds" (1728) [see detail in **Figure 2**]. During Emperor Yongzheng's reign, Castiglione worked intensively on flowers, landscapes, and birds and other animals, taking each subject to new poetic and technical heights along the way.

During this process, Castiglione's works on portraiture also attained incredible realism never before seen in China, despite the challenge of not being permitted to employ chiaroscuro (light and shadow) techniques,

---

1. Matteo Ricci introduced several instruments to the Court during his pioneering work in Beijing, including the clavichord (*gukin*). He also composed eight moral poems titled *Songs for Western Keyboard* (*Xi qin Quyi*), each being rendered as a musical composition using counterpoint. Today only Matteo's text survives, but not his music. Ricci also introduced many religious paintings which did not resonate with the Chinese at the time.

2. Marco Musillo. *Reconciling Two Careers: The Jesuit Memoir of Guiseppe Castiglione*, 2008.

as Chinese aesthetics during the Qing period considered such uses of shadow in portraiture as morally inferior. Even with this restraint, Castiglione was able to convey a deep realism and spirit in the personalities of his figures, discussed more fully below.

Castiglione, following in the tradition of Leonardo da Vinci, is also credited with producing the first treatise on perspective in China, *The Science of Vision* (Shixue) in 1729. He designed many murals in the Forbidden City for Emperor Qianlong using the *trompe l'oeil* effect called *quadratura*, which was popularized in European cathedrals and theatres [**Figure 3**]. Castiglione's collaborator in the publication of Shixue was a brilliant Chinese mathematician, painter and government official named Nian Xiyao, who wrote in the book's preface:

> China has cultivated a great tradition of depicting nature in landscape paintings but neglected the accurate representation of projection and the measurement of buildings and implements. If one desires to depict these objects correctly, one must use the western technique.

Rites Controversy: Threat to Renaissance Thought in China

The close collaboration between the Qing Court and the Jesuit Fathers was fundamentally destroyed by a process known as the Rites Controversy, which began during the reign of Kangxi and came to its drastic end during the reign of his grandson, Qianlong. The fault lies entirely with the Venetian faction within the Church in Rome. Since the time of Matteo Ricci—the first to recognize the profound

Figure 1. Castiglione's "Gathering of Auspicious Signs" (1723).

Figure 2. Detail of Castiglione's "One Hundred Steeds."

nature of the Confucian tradition, both in its philosophic and religious nature, and in its embrace of a scientific outlook toward the development of man and nature—he and the Jesuits who followed him over the next century were given leading positions in the Court, especially in the Bureau of Astronomy, which played a central role in Chinese society.

Gottfried Leibniz, whose correspondence with several Jesuit Fathers in China led him to publish detailed comparative studies of Christian and Confucian beliefs and practices in his *Novissima Sinica* (1697), described Kangxi as a monarch "who almost exceeds human heights of greatness, being a god-like mortal, ruling by a nod of his head, who, however, is educated to virtue and wisdom ..., thereby earning his

Figure 3. One of the many examples of the "trompe l'oeil effect," by Castiglione.

right to rule." Leibniz wrote, anticipating the New Silk Road:

> I consider it a singular plan of the fates that human cultivation and refinement should today be concentrated, as it were, in the two extremes of our continent, in Europe and in China, which adorns the Orient as Europe does the opposite edge of the Earth. Perhaps Supreme Providence has ordained such an arrangement, so that as the most cultivated and distant peoples stretch out their arms to each other, those in between may gradually be brought to a better way of life. I do not think it an accident that the Russians, whose vast realm connects Europe with China and who hold sway over the deep barbarian lands of the North by the shore of the frozen ocean, should be led to the emulation of our ways through the strenuous efforts of their present ruler [Peter I].[3]

In 1692, Kangxi issued an edict granting all Christians the right to teach and preach, and to bring Chinese subjects into the Catholic Church, requiring only that civil servants, who were chosen for their positions based on national examinations in Confucian moral and social teachings, maintain moral allegiance to the Confucian principles and continue to perform the rites and ceremonies appropriate to their offices.

A debate ensued in Rome, with the Jesuits being accused of condoning "pagan" practices and supposedly obfuscating the Confucian views regarding God. (See "Matteo Ricci, the Grand Design, and the Disaster of the 'Rites Controversy'.") Over the next fifty years, this faction, knowing little or nothing about China or the Confucian ideas, argued that a Chinese subject must renounce Confucianism before becoming a Christian. It succeeded in convincing several Popes to issue Papal Bulls against Christian adherence to Confucian beliefs and rites. Since the adherence to Confucian moral and social teachings were the basis of government service, these dictates from Rome essentially demanded a revolt against the government and the peace of the state by Christian recruits.

Kangxi had no choice but to expel the Christian missionaries in 1720, although he allowed several of the leading scientific advisors to retain positions in the Astronomy and Engineering bureaus—and he allowed Giuseppe Castiglione to remain in the Court to continue his painting and teaching.

More than a century of collaboration between Renaissance science and culture in the West and that of Confucian China in the East was drastically and tragically curtailed. (The scholar Nathan Sivin has argued forcefully that this era of cooperation had witnessed a true scientific revolution in China.) The pace of the dramatic scientific and economic progress within China gradually slowed over time. In the West, the imperial forces centered in Venice and later in the Anglo-Dutch Empire asserted their power over the humanist forces that had supported cooperation between East and West. By the 19th Century, British gunboats, loaded not only with weapons, but also with opium from British India, invaded and conquered the weakened forces in China, unleashing the "Century of Humiliation" of imperial occupation and forced legalization of opium in China.

The Kangxi Emperor (1661-1722)

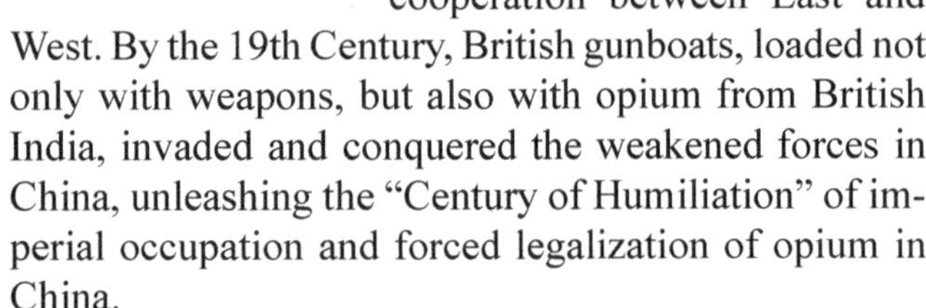

Qianlong Emperor: Castiglione's Protector and Patron

The progress made during the Kangxi reign, due in no small part to the collaboration with the Jesuit Fathers, was in part sustained under the following reigns of Yongzheng and Qianlong (reigned 1722-35 and 1735-1796, respectively), both of whom continued to cooperate with the few Jesuits who had been allowed to remain in China—including Giuseppe Castiglione. Qianlong, the Qing dynasty's 4th and longest reigning Emperor, saw himself walking in his grandfather's

---

3. G.W. Leibniz. Preface to the *Novissima Sinica* (News from China), translated by Daniel J. Cook and Henry Rosemont, Jr., in their *Gottfried Wilhelm Leibniz: Writings on China,* Open Court, 1998, pp. 45-46. For the full story of Leibniz's extraordinary design and efforts to unite Europe and China, see "The Leibnizian Roots of Eurasian Integration," by Jason Ross, *Executive Intelligence Review,* April 29, 2016.

footsteps as an ecumenical unifier of the diverse ethnicities, religions and language groups in China.

Qianlong also had to resist efforts by his more radical advisors, who demanded that all Jesuits be expelled from the Imperial Board of Astronomy which they had led since the early days of the Qing Dynasty. He also promoted Castiglione to third civil official rank and Vice President of the Six Boards.[4] The Emperor also sponsored the western-eastern fusion of the visual arts and architecture in ways never before seen. The National Palace Museum of Taipei features the following description of Qianlong's outlook on the arts:

> Qianlong, who perceived detailed, naturalistic painting as a means of propagating the magnificence of the Qing empire was a particularly strong proponent of this mixing of eastern and western artistic styles.

One of Castiglione's close allies in Beijing was Ferdinand Augustin Hallerstein (1703-1774), who served as a leading diplomat between the East and West and was the head of the Imperial Board of Astronomy from 1746-1774. Hallerstein's letters provide insight into the tense atmosphere of the Court and the Emperor's resistance to the anti-Christian pressures being applied by his advisors. Early in the Emperor's reign, all efforts made by the missionaries to speak with the Emperor and plead for leniency had been blocked by the court eunuchs and mandarins. Hallerstein documented that a memorial letter of leniency had been presented by Castiglione to the Emperor in 1736, in the following account:

> The Emperor came as usual to sit by him and watch him paint. The Brother laid down his brush and, suddenly assuming a sad expression, fell to his knees and after uttering a few words Sacred Law drew from his breast our Memorial wrapped in yellow silk. The eunuchs of the presence trembled at this Brother's audacity, for he had concealed his purpose from them. However, the Emperor listened to him calmly and said to him in a kindly way: "I have not condemned your religion; I have simply forbidden the people of the Banners [referring to officials and military forces] to embrace it." At the same time he signed to the eunuchs to receive the Memorial and turning to Castiglione he added: "I shall read it, do not worry, and go on painting."[5]

It was in this same year that China's first painting academy was established, which strongly promoted the Xianfa style and Castiglione was made "official court painter."

Governance and Art

Since Castiglione's art is very much connected to the governance of China, it is important to briefly look at the political environment shaping his art from several angles.

After putting down Mongol uprisings in 1755-59 and extending the empire's territories to include Tibet and some areas now in Central Asia, the Qianlong Emperor did not enslave the Mongol Buddhist or Zunghar (central Asian) peoples, but rather worked to build, beautify and protect their temples, mosques and other cultural treasures. In mastering their languages, and even adopting many of their customs as his own, the Emperor, who was fluent in 5 languages, described his approach to cultural diplomacy in the following terms:

> When the rota of Mongols, Muslims and Tibetans come every year to the capital for an audience I use their own languages and do not rely on an interpreter ... to express the idea of conquering by kindness.

In the various portraits which Castiglione was commissioned to paint of the Qianlong Emperor for display in the various regions of China, the Emperor consciously projected himself differently to each constituency. The National Palace Museum of Taipei described the strategy thus:

> To the Tibetans, Qianlong portrayed himself as a re-incarnation of one of the most important bodhisattvas of Tibetan Buddhism, Manjusri; for the Mongols, he took on the role of a Steppe prince

---

4. This was the highest rank ever achieved by a Jesuit. See Friederike Biebl, "The Magnificence of the Qing—European Art on the Jesuit Mission in China," 2014.

5. Natasa Vampelj Suhadolnic. "Ferdinand Augustin Hallerstein on Giuseppe Castiglione's Art," 2015.

Figure 4. Three portraits by Castiglione of the Qianlang Emperor, as he presented himself to various constituencies: in Manchu warrior armor (left), as formal Han royalty (middle), and as the Buddhist Mañjuśrī (right).

who understood their steppe traditions; and to the Han Chinese he portrayed himself as a scholar and a great patron of Chinese Learning and art. [**Figure 4**]

Most importantly, however, the Emperor saw himself not as an elite dictator, but as a humble servant. In many of his portraits, Qianlong ensured that Castiglione portrayed him with his family, studying paintings or practicing calligraphy, or hunting deer, rather than in formal imperial styles. [**Figure 5**]

Emperor Qianlong promoted a Confucian policy of political harmony through the advancement of arts and culture. For this reason, Qianlong loved his friend Castiglione more than all other missionaries and advisors, maintaining him as the official court painter during his entire reign, with Castiglione being the only foreigner ever permitted into the bedchambers of the Emperor and his wife in order to paint their portraits.[6] He made

______

6. In an anonymous, unpublished biography of Castiglione written soon after his death, the anecdote of the Emperor's admiration for the painter is described, as well as Castiglione's humility and disdain for honors: "Since he was a child, he was an admirer of Castiglione and developed a great love and filial affection for him. As soon as he became

Figure 5. Two Castiglione portraits of the Qianlong Emperor: in his study (left, date unknown); and in a detail with the Royal Children (right, 1736-37).

Figure 6a. Ruins of the Emperor Qianlong's Old Summer Palace.

Figure 6b. Artist's rendering of the Old Summer Palace.

Castiglione Administrator of Imperial Parks and commissioned him to design the decorations and western-styled pavilions inside the gardens of the Old Summer Palace, the Yuanmingyuan, in 1747. The British made sure to destroy these works during the Second Opium War of 1860 and only relics remain today, although artistic reconstructions do exist which feature a glorious image of a classical fusion of eastern and western architecture [**Figure 6**].

When Castiglione died on July 17, 1766 in Beijing, the Emperor personally wrote his obituary, erected a tombstone and ensured that he was buried alongside the two greatest Jesuit missionaries who paved the way for a new paradigm of universal renaissance thinking, Matteo Ricci and Johann Adam Schall von Bell.

With the destructive consequences of the Opium Wars and the foreign imperial control over China, Xianfa ceased to be practiced and has been largely forgotten. However, with President Xi Jinping leading a new era of ecumenicism and cultural exchange under the New Silk Road, the spirit of Castiglione and other great renaissance visionaries can finally be revived and taken to a new level.

Let us close with the wise words of Helga Zepp-LaRouche, who summarized this potential in her April 14, 2017 speech to a Schiller Institute conference, under the title, "East and West: A Dialogue of Great Cultures":

The Confucian tradition is experiencing a great renaissance in China right now, led by President Xi Jinping, who has made it a point that Confucian teaching must be taught on all levels of society. We could turn back to the European high tradition at will. We could go back to Plato, the Classical Greeks, the Italian Renaissance, the German Classical period. And this is the European culture which is the New Paradigm of the New Silk Road, and if it is revived with a dialogue of culture with it, then at any time we can make it alive and with it a new Renaissance. If each nation and each culture makes alive again their highest cultural achievements, presenting to themselves and other nations their best aspect, it is certain a new renaissance will come—seizing upon the best from universal history, but beyond that, enthusiastically creating new corresponding concepts for mankind achieving maturity.

---

the Emperor, he could not stand the fact that the worthy old man did not have any honors, so he decreed that he would enter the Order of Mandarins. [...] A lot of people started to congratulate him openly on what they thought was a settled fact, but the virtuous old man abhorred these kinds of honors, [...]. So while asking God for what he had to do to avoid those honors [...] he looked unusually sad so that his friends took it as a clear sign of his unwillingness to accept such a favor: a clear sign indeed also for the Emperor, who as he did not want to afflict the very person he wanted to gratify, recalled the decree, something which rarely happens. Castiglione's humility had prevailed." (Musillo, *op. cit.,* p. 54)

FEB. 6, 2005

The Global Option for this Emergency: Beyond Westphalia Now

by Lyndon H. LaRouche, Jr.

The discussions to be held in Northern Virginia [Schiller Institute conference, February 19-20, 2005] will address certain included challenges which are of existential importance for the continued existence of the U.S. republic. Our role in meeting these challenges is now a unique capability, and therefore a unique responsibility, for reviving the kind of U.S. leadership for today which had been manifest under President Franklin Roosevelt prior to his most untimely death. This involves a capability which is inherent in both the unique characteristics of our republic, and the special influence which the presently U.S.-dollar-dominated, but collapsing, present world monetary-financial institutions have for determining the immediate period's well-being of mankind as a whole.

As I have argued on earlier occasions, the world as a whole has reached the point of development, at which the assured continuation of civilized life on this planet requires us to reject the follies of experiments in so-called "globalization," in favor of a system of respectively sovereign nation-states which would have established a form of planetary system of cooperation. This would be the establishment of a form which is most fairly described as a realization of the same aims and principles which were implicit in that 1648 Treaty of Westphalia which brought to an end both the inherent evils of ultramontane feudalism, and ended, for that time, that impulse toward religious warfare which has returned to much of the world today: an impulse presented under the twin lunatic guises of so-called "religious fundamentalism" or racism, a moral degeneration presently integral to those follies of so-called "global-ization," which threaten the continued existence of civilized life on this planet today.

As I have emphasized on earlier occasions, the pivotal challenge to be recognized today, is the fact that we have reached the point that civilized life requires a forceful suppression of efforts to establish an ultramontane or other mode of imperial control over the planet as a whole, a control being attempted now through the rise in the roles of speculative monopolies in control of essential so-called "raw materials." There is no intrinsic shortage of necessary raw materials, if sovereign nations cooperate to develop the raw materials of this planet in ways which ensure an increase in organized supply adequate for the inevitably growing requirements of all nations.

This is a point in world financial-monetary, as well as physical-economic development of nations, at which the assurance of both fair prices and adequate supply for what we presently view as the raw materials needs of nations, means that orderly economic relations among sovereign nation-states, require establishing long-term agreements under a new system of fixed exchange-rates, a system in which the stability of supply of needed raw materials at fair prices is the primary factor of a global system of long-term capital formation, through cooperative management to this effect over forward intervals of approximately two generations.

At the present moment, the world is gripped by the effects of foolish decisions which undermined and destroyed the fixed-exchange-rate monetary system which had been established at the close of the 1939-1945 warfare. Increasingly wild-eyed financial specu-

"*There is no intrinsic shortage of necessary raw materials, if sovereign nations cooperate to develop the raw materials of this planet in ways which ensure an increase in organized supply adequate for the inevitably growing requirements of all nations.*" *Here, an oil refinery.*

lation, is capped by the sheer lunacy of a financial-monetary system rife with madcap financial derivatives speculation. Most of the nominal financial claims associated with the speculative orgies of the 1971-2004 interval could never be satisfied. Yet, to make a safe transition from the present homicidal lunacy of the world's current monetary-financial system, we must maintain the security of a system for those long-term monetary-financial assets which are expressed as essential forms of present and future public and private improvements in the physical-capital preconditions of civilized life of nations and their peoples.

To establish that needed reform of the world's monetary-financial system, it will be necessary to predicate the security of essential forms of capitalization of such long-term assets by pledging the security of financial capital against a program of vigorous development of the essential basic raw materials available to a community of nations, each and all engaged in common goals of improvement of the productive powers of labor and conditions of life for generations still to come.

This consideration of the implications of raw-materials development and management, provides the principled basis for a long-term, fixed-exchange-rate system.

In general, this means establishing a new monetary system under the renewed principle of the Treaty of Westphalia, as applied to these present circumstances and their challenges. It requires little more than a fair estimate of the situation to suggest, that in taking such steps for progress under conditions of the ongoing general breakdown crisis of the world's present, self-doomed monetary-financial system, we must recognize that we are embarked on the implied measures of general reorganization of the world, a reorganization whose initial phase will be not less than two generations, which is to say, in terms of requirements of modern society and its technology, two generations aggregating to about 50 years. Agreements to such effects must be the premise for reconciling the relations between valid existing capital assets and the terms of repayment of capital obligations, that over an initial base period of about 50 years.

The only present alternative to such measures of reform, would be chaos, and, most probably, a prolonged new dark age for humanity as a whole. At this very moment, the world as a whole is at the brink of such a global, chain-reaction collapse.

The political situation thus confronting the participants in that meeting may be summarized as follows.

The Political Crisis

Especially since the first year of the George W. Bush, Jr. Administration, more and more of the world at large has tended more and more toward the wish that the U.S.'s own self-inflicted crises would soon eliminate the U.S.A. as a dominant factor in the foreseeable future of the planet. Such wishful views delude those who believe that the ruin of the U.S.'s influence would thus free the rest of the world to go its own way. That increasingly widespread wish, must be denounced as a delusion. It is a belief whose effects would be the ruin of civilization as a whole for a long time to come.

The post-1989-1991 influence of the U.S.A. as what some regard as a self-estimated monopole of world destiny, is exaggerated in many ways. The U.S. role today is merely that of an instrument of the same Anglo-Dutch Liberal imperialism which the U.S. fought, for its independence and Constitution, during 1776-1789, against the Anglo-Dutch Liberal-imperialist system from which President Franklin Roosevelt's leadership had temporarily freed the U.S., until the virtually treasonous monetary reforms led by the relevant Anglo-American financial powers of 1971-1972. Nonetheless, although the U.S. control over the present monetary-financial system is widely misunderstood by popular opinion around the world today, the outreach of the present, post-1991, U.S.-dollar-denominated form of Anglo-Dutch Liberal world system, has such a dominant role within the world's present continuation of that world's monetary-financial system, that, in the present crisis-circumstances, the fate of humanity as a whole depends upon certain leading, dollar-based remedial initiatives by the U.S. government itself.

Thus, although it is the presently degenerating, Anglo-Dutch Liberal system of 1763-1914 which is again ruling the post-1971 world of today, today's form of that world system as a whole now requires initiatives, to create a new financial-monetary system, under which the world as a whole depends on certain global initiatives of monetary-financial reform which could not be introduced without the role of certain specific kinds of initiatives which must come from inside the U.S.A. itself.

For example:

Were the U.S.A. government so recklessly foolish as to tolerate George "Hjalmar Schacht" Shultz's Pinochet model for raiding the U.S. Social Security system of trillions of dollars, the situation for both the U.S. dollar and the world monetary-financial system generally would become immediately hopeless. Take into account the pattern of spiralling fiscal and current-accounts-deficits of the U.S. dollar, and the role of that dollar in defining presently, the financial-derivatives-rotted-out fiscal and monetary systems of the world at large. The chain-reaction effects of the consequent, already looming combined, U.S. fiscal and current-accounts deficit, would not merely sink the U.S. dollar, but this collapse of the dollar would have immediate, devastating effects throughout Eurasia and beyond. No part of the world as a whole is presently situated to avoid being sucked into the global chaos which such a development would ensure.

While no one could possibly calculate in advance exactly how bad the effects of the now onrushing general monetary-financial collapse would be on the planet as a whole, it is certain that the results of failure to take the options which I have proposed would be both more or less awful, and assuredly planet-wide.

Thus, a presently most probable, early collapse of the U.S. dollar system as such, has effects with which no part of the world could cope effectively, except by aid of certain political initiatives from the U.S.A. itself. The measures to be taken are of a nature which could not be possible within the framework of the post-1971 model of that Anglo-Dutch Liberal form of post-FDR monetarist system, which came into being through the keystone role of the U.S. Nixon Administration's George Shultz and his confederates. Only a prompt return to the principles of the American System as defined by President Franklin Roosevelt's leadership at the founding Bretton Woods conference, could provide the needed foundation for the urgently needed form of programmed stabilization of dollar-linked debt, a form of stabilization of fungible long-term debt-capital needed for the situation facing the coming two generations of this planet at large.

Therefore, the pivotal point to be stressed in all discussion of this matter must be the following:

In this circumstance, only actions which stabilize the U.S. dollar's unevadable present role as presently denominated, WORLD RESERVE CURRENCY could avert the threatened plunge of the planet into a global catastrophe comparable to Europe's 14-Century "New Dark Age." What is required is emergency reorganization of the present world monetary system as in a bankruptcy-reorganization conducted by cooperation among certain sovereign governments of nation-states, especially the leading nation-states of North America and Eurasia.

The success of any attempted such rescue-action depends upon the ability to freeze certain kinds of both presently existing, and newly added long-term, dollar-denominated physical assets at defensible, relatively fixed financial prices, prices which can be made to hold for not less than the long-term interval of a quarter to half a century. This latter condition must be secured to provide a credible basis for a return of a global, fixed-exchange-rate monetary system comparable to the

The greatest intellectual obstacle to understanding the required modes of emergency reform to be made immediately ahead, is the failure of most, including so-called professional economists inside and outside the U.S.A., to recognize the deep roots of the intellectual incompetence which allowed the change from President Franklin Roosevelt's Bretton Woods system to the present floating-exchange-rate monetary system to emerge under ideologues such as the U.S. Nixon Administration's chief "Chicago School" ideologue George Shultz.

intent expressed by U.S. President Franklin Roosevelt's leading role in creating the original Bretton Woods System.

The new monetary system, so grounded, must be intended, by design, to provide support for a newly expanded system of long-term treaty-agreements, especially agreements focussed upon cooperation of the U.S.A. with the growing cooperative development trends among leading nation-states of the Eurasian continent. Without such a programmed form of long-term cooperation of the U.S.A. with the kind of cooperative development within Eurasia which I have specified as in the form of cooperation of western and central Europe with a Russia-China-India Productive Triangle, no practicable solution for the planet as a whole exists for the next two or more generations to come.

The Bretton Woods System

The greatest intellectual obstacle to understanding the required modes of emergency reform to be made immediately ahead, is the failure of most, including so-called professional economists inside and outside the U.S.A., to recognize the deep roots of the intellectual incompetence which allowed the change from President Franklin Roosevelt's Bretton Woods system to the present floating-exchange-rate monetary system to emerge under ideologues such as the U.S. Nixon Administration's chief "Chicago School" ideologue George Shultz.

This is not to go so far as to argue that most leading economists of the world's recent generations have been simply stupid. Some economists and financial specialists are skilled in their own way; their fault, in allowing the degeneration of the world's monetary-financial system to go as far as it has, has been, among both Soviet and so-called Western economists. that they locate their skills in working within the existing system, without due consideration for those flawed underlying axioms which have led, repeatedly, to the great crises of modern European civilization (in particular). Therefore, for reason of that kind of intellectual shortcoming, they limit their proposed reforms to changes within the bounds of those philosophically reductionist, empiricist or related axiomatic assumptions which have, in fact, been the root of every major economic and strategic crisis which globally extended modern European civilization has experienced since the Fall of Constantinople.

Contrary to those trends in so-called expert opinion, my own, essentially Platonic views on the subject of systems of physical economy, are those which I adopted largely as echoes of my reading of the work of Gottfried Leibniz. For me, European civilization, in the nobler sense of the term, is distinguished by that struggle to define society in terms of those creative powers of the individual mind which distinguish the human individual absolutely from the beasts. It is those discoveries of universal physical and Classical artistic principle, which history associates with the legacy of Thales, Solon of Athens, Pythagoras, Socrates, Plato, et al., which define the meaning of the terms "the human individual" and "society" for the purposes of competent statecraft, then as now. That is to emphasize that it is that sovereign creative power of hypothesis-making, through which experimentally validated universal principles of the universe are discovered and applied, that distinguishes man from the beasts.

From this vantage-point, the evils of European history, such as the reductionism of the Greek Sophists and their like, the Romans, and the imperial ultramontanism of the Venetian financier oligarchy and its Norman Crusader allies, is a crime against that feature of the nature of man which sets the human individual apart from the beasts. Thus, for us, the Classical Humanists so defined, it is the development of that quality of the

The IMF Executive Board, meeting in Washington. The U.S. role today is merely that of an instrument of the Anglo-Dutch Liberal system—the same imperial, ultramontane system against which the United States fought for its independence during 1776-1789.

human individual which must be chosen as the purpose of society, and the standard of practice by which society, its laws, and its customs are to be judged as good or bad.

Thus, for us, the modern Classical Humanists, the 15th-Century European Renaissance, as marked by that great ecumenical Council of Florence which liberated Europe from the legacy of the Venetian-Norman ultramontane tyranny, is also the Renaissance which built the foundation of all that is good in globally extended modern European civilization. That is the good for which we have been forced to struggle against the Spanish Inquisition, the waves of religious warfare which that Inquisition unleashed, and against evil Venice's successor, the tradition of that Anglo-Dutch Liberal financier-oligarchical imperialism which has been the dominant influence in the world during most of the period since the February 1763 Treaty of Paris. The creation of the U.S. republic must be recognized as the leading revolt against that Anglo-Dutch Liberal tyranny from within Europe, during the time of the American Revolution of 1776-1789, a revolt which was also expressed, most notably, under great U.S. patriots of that tradition, such as Presidents Abraham Lincoln and Franklin Roosevelt.

Unfortunately, the anti-Roosevelt, factional allies of Winston Churchill within the Anglo-American war-time alliance, used the occasion of the death of Franklin Roosevelt to subvert, and rapidly reverse the great achievements under Roosevelt. Thus, from the death of that President Franklin Roosevelt, until the typical role of George Shultz in the wrecking of the Bretton Woods system under President Nixon, it was the lingering benefits of Roosevelt's assertion of the American System of political-economy, the anti-British Bretton Woods system, which played the leading progressive role in promoting world economic development during the 1945-1971 interval.

The attempt to define a post-Soviet world history as a U.S. strategic monopole has promoted the widespread delusion—among those who wished to be deluded, in Europe and elsewhere, that the present world system is an American imperial system. On the contrary, it is a reassertion of the Fabian Liberal imperialism of the followers of Anglo-Dutch Liberalism's Lord Shelburne, but under circumstances in which the wildly speculative, U.S.-based factions of today's world-wide Anglo-Dutch monetary-system, have come to play a dominant political role of control within the world's present form of imperial role of the Anglo-Dutch Liberal tradition as a whole. Thus, the remedy for the world at large, becomes now the breaking of the grip of that international financier-oligarchical faction over the control of the present world monetary-financial system, a break which, by the nature of current realities, must be made initially from within the U.S. itself.

In harsh reality, such a needed rescue of the world from the present monetary-financial crisis, could occur only in the form of a return to the specific principles of the original Bretton Woods system. That initiative must come from within the U.S.A., or it will not come at all.

It is time to dump the farcical assertion that the fixed-exchange-rate of Franklin Roosevelt's International Monetary System, was the adoption of a "Keynesian" system. As John Maynard Keynes wrote in the special, German introduction to the first, Berlin publication of his General Theory, Keynes' system was, as he correctly claimed, most agreeable with a Germany under Nazism. Keynes saw himself as a central banker within the bounds of a form of international financier-oligarchy of the same type as his Synarchist International contemporaries of the 1920s and 1930s. Roosevelt was

America's first Treasury Secretary, Alexander Hamilton. In today's crisis conditions, only actions which stabilize the U.S. dollar's role as a world reserve currency could avert the threatened plunge of the planet into a global catastrophe.

an advocate of the Hamiltonian national banking implicit in the U.S. Federal Constitution and the leading adversary of the Synarchist International financier bloc of that time.

The bankruptcy of all of the U.S.A.'s western and central European rivals under the processes of 1922-1945, created the opportunity to assert the primacy of the U.S. fixed-exchange-rate system, and to impose the principles of that system for what proved to be a temporary subjugation of what had been the 1763-1933, global imperial supremacy of the Anglo-Dutch Liberal financier-oligarchical system. Although U.S. President Truman did not wait for President Franklin Roosevelt's burial, to go over into the anti-American camp of Winston Churchill's financier-oligarchy imperialism, it was not until the Nixon Administration, under the guidance of technicians such as George Shultz, Henry A. Kissinger, et al., that the Anglo-Dutch Liberal faction was able to rid itself of Roosevelt's American System, by

creating that floating-exchange-rate system whose internal logic has brought the world now to a state far worse than merely general bankruptcy, to the condition of a presently onrushing, general breakdown-crisis of the present world system.

The outcome of these leading developments of the just-past 20th Century, produced the anomalous fateful state of world affairs today.

What Nixon's advisors, such as Shultz, and also relatively lower-ranking figures such as Henry A. Kissinger did, was to place what had become the U.S.-dollar-denominated system under the control of an international financier-oligarchical cabal, in which relevant U.S. elements were merely a leading financier interest. The result of the changes in the system, which had begun with the United Kingdom's first Harold Wilson government, and continued through the sweeping changes in monetary-system architecture over the 1971-1982 interval, has been to use the U.S. dollar-denominated international monetary system, to built up a mountain of debt within what has been chiefly a dollar-denominated system, a grotesque caricature of the pre-1933 Anglo-Dutch Liberal global imperium.

Thus, since the major portion of financial assets of the world today are denominated in IMF dollars, and since the hyperinflationary build-up of short-term investments in debt has come to vastly outweigh long-term financial capital holdings in real capital holdings, and that at a greatly accelerated rate under President George W. Bush, the presently onrushing collapse of the U.S. dollar has created a situation in which only a reform of the U.S. dollar in accord with the precedent of Roosevelt's Bretton Woods design would permit the kind of reorganization in bankruptcy to which the entire world system must be subjected today.

It is only through the recapture of the political leadership of the U.S. by forces dedicated to the Roosevelt legacy of the original Bretton Woods system, that the world-wide behavior of the U.S. dollar can be brought into conformity with the kind of required reform on which long-term stability of fungible forms of debt-capital can be organized for the planet as a whole.

This does not mean U.S. imperialism; but, exactly the contrary. It means that the initiative of the U.S. as a sovereign nation-state republic, is crucial for any attempted reorganization of the world monetary-financial system. It is chiefly the world's U.S.-dollar-denominated

Army Corps of Engineers.

"The great and crucial portion of the new capital-formation in basic economic infrastructure, will be as international capital associated with long-term treaty agreements among sovereign nation-states." Here, a U.S. Army Corps of Engineers project for construction of a retaining wall at Sargent Beach, Texas, on the Gulf of Mexico.

formation is not to be limited to the public sector's infrastructure, but the role of public investment in infrastructure must be a leading feature of long-term capital formation in all productive and related sectors. By combining the worthy long-term bonded and related infrastructural and kindred private debt of today, with a vast, fresh generation of new fixed-exchange rate, long-term capital in basic economic infrastructure, a successful reorganization of the presently bankrupt system suddenly becomes feasible.

The great and crucial portion of the new capital-formation in basic economic infrastructure, will be as international capital associated with long-term treaty agreements among sovereign nation-states. The term of the bulk of this new capital will span a quarter to a half century, as the case of Europe's participation in the development of China attests. This gives a powerful new depth of meaning to the principle, of "advantage of the other," of the 1648 Treaty of Westphalia.

Nations must be perfectly sovereign, but they share a common interest in promoting the advantage of the other. Otherwise, there is no likelihood of any nation's recovery from the presently onrushing crisis.

Typical is the present emergence of a situation in Eurasia, in which the prosperity of each economy will depend upon the successful long-term capital formation of the other. That is already the long-term trend emerging in political-economic relations between western and central Europe. The pivotal role of Russia between the emerging economies of Asia and the well-being of the states of western and central Europe, typifies the situation.

It can be done, but it could be done only under the pressures of a global crisis as immediately menacing as the situation now. Necessity will be the forceful mother of the needed invention. Nations will swim in the waters of a new economic system, not because of a zeal for swimming, but because they perceive that it is necessary to swim, if one is to survive.

financial debt, which must be reorganized, even that debt held as a sovereign asset of other states. The system required is a return to the principle of the original Bretton Woods design; but, the system so established must be a partnership among respectively sovereign nation-states. The U.S. role in this reform will be pivotal; without that role, played as I have just implied, there is no reasonable hope that the world could be saved from a relatively immediate collapse into a prolonged, planetary, new dark age, comparable to, but worse than that of Europe's 14th Century.

The differences between the IMF as designed at the point of President Franklin Roosevelt's untimely death, and the indicated return to a semblance of the original, fixed-exchange-rate form of IMF system, require that the state of harmonious conflict prescribed for the original Bretton Woods institution at its best performance, must be superseded by the application of the model of the 1648 Treaty of Westphalia.

This reference to the Treaty of Westphalia does not mean a configuration of political sentiments. It points to the importance of the needed creation of vast masses of long-term international debt, within a fixed-exchange-rate system, for, chiefly, the vast physical investments in long-term basic economic infrastructure. This capital

www.ingramcontent.com/pod-product-compliance
Lightning Source LLC
Chambersburg PA
CBHW080245260726

48658CB00008B/3240